# 32
## Christians Who Changed Their World

# 32
# CHRISTIANS WHO
# CHANGED
# THEIR WORLD

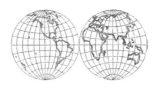

*Glenn S. Sunshine*

CANON PRESS

MOSCOW, IDAHO

Published by Canon Press
P. O. Box 8729, Moscow, Idaho 83843
800-488-2034 | www.canonpress.com

Cover design by James Engerbretson
Interior design by Valerie Anne Bost
Printed in the United States of America

Unless otherwise indicated, all Scripture quotations are from the King James Version. All Bible quotations marked ESV are from the English Standard Version, copyright © 2001 by Crossway Bibles, a division of Good News Publishers. Used by permission.

*Library of Congress Cataloguing-in-Publication data is forthcoming.*

23 24 25 26 27 28 29 30 31    10 9 8 7 6 5 4 3 2 1

To the memory of my friend and mentor Charles W. Colson,
and to T. M. Moore, Principal of the Fellowship of Ailbe and
former Director of the Centurions Program,
who together set me on the course to write this book.

# CONTENTS

# PREFACE

NEAR THE END OF THE BIBLE'S "HALL
of Faith" chapter, the author of Hebrews realizes he's running out of time. He also wants us to know about others who
deserve a place in this list of the faithful ... the ones who
experienced miraculous healings ... those who won unexpected victories ... those raised from the dead.

And there were others, too, who were "tortured ... [and]
suffered mocking and flogging ... even chains and imprisonment. They were stoned, they were sawn in two, they
were killed with the sword ... destitute, afflicted, mistreated"
(11:35–37).

It is a bit discomforting just how seamlessly the list
moves from miracles to persecution. The reader is offered no
explanation for this. No distinction is made between those
who won and those who lost, those whose faith enabled

amazing things and those whose faith precipitated their demise. There is no consolation offered, at least not in any temporal outcomes. All that we are told is that they belong to a distinct group of people, one "of whom the world is not worthy" (v. 38).

Imagine how long this same list is today. The faithful now include people across centuries, continents, vocations, and cultures. There are pastors, evangelists, sculptors, parents, entrepreneurs, activists, warriors, strategists, inventors, servants, rulers, innovators, educators, children, authors, painters, athletes, presidents, beggars, healers, storytellers, academics, practitioners, politicians, administrators, builders, peasants, accountants, and those from any other category of human activity that one could imagine. They are proof of the Church universal, which Christ, who is Lord of all, promised to build. He kept that promise, and because He did, history is full of people from every tongue, tribe, nation, and language who have declared that "every square inch" of the cosmos is His.

In a speech recorded in Acts 17, Paul described God to a group of Athenian philosophers. In it, he offered a particular detail, having to do with God's interaction within human history, that is not articulated in the same way anywhere else in Scripture. God determines the exact time and exact place for each human being to live. Or in Paul's words, their "allotted periods and the boundaries of their dwelling place" (v. 26). Such a detail was especially important for this particular audience, which, according to Luke, consisted of Epicureans and Stoics.

Each of these philosophical groups held distinct and differing views about the relationship between the gods and the world. The Epicureans believed that the gods were no longer interested or engaged in the affairs of men, so humans lived without divine accountability. Stoics believed, in contrast, that most aspects of our lives were determined by the gods. Human freedom was, largely, illusory.

In a Christian view, God has complete oversight over His world, but not in a way that negates human freedom or action. He determines our time and place, Paul told the pagans, so that we could, in fact, respond to Him. Our response to His presence in the world has real meaning. Even more, because God Himself, in Christ, entered time and place, not only is He not aloof from the human condition, He experienced it Himself. All of this is part of the larger story of the cosmos in which, ultimately, His will will be done on earth, where we are, as it is in heaven, from which He reigns forever and ever.

For years, Dr. Glenn Sunshine has studied and told of faithful believers who not only believed this Story but lived, in their time and their place, as if it were true. Most were not Christian "professionals." In other words, they were not employed as pastors or missionaries. Instead, they worked across various cultural spheres as if Christian truth mattered as much there as in any church. They sought to educate because they believed God is truth. They sought to liberate, because they knew every person bears God's image and that truth sets us free. They sought to create, because in creating we worship the Creator. They sought to alleviate suffering, because God had, originally, created the world good. They fought injustice because God is just and wants justice in His world. They lived as if Christ is King, because they knew He is.

Some of these "Christians Who Changed the World" will be familiar, but many won't be. That only underscores what we must always remember about changing the world: our job is to be faithful to the fullness of the truth and reign of Jesus Christ. The men and women in the following pages were faithful, sometimes in small ways, but were used by God in the unfolding of His grand Story and for the good of many.

May we never get over the fact that He allows us to participate as Kingdom agents, playing parts in His Story that actually matter. And may we never forget that He is both the source and the goal of any good work, in every area of life. As T.S. Eliot put it, "For us there is only the trying. The rest is none of our business."

JOHN STONESTREET

# INTRODUCTION

THIS BOOK BEGAN WITH A LECTURE I gave for the Centurions Program, now known as the Colson Fellows, under Chuck Colson. I was assigned the topic "Christians Who Changed Their World" for a talk to be given just before the graduating class was commissioned. That was bad enough: they had finished the program and I doubted they wanted a content-heavy lecture. Further, I knew Chuck, so I knew he expected me to do William Wilberforce, his personal hero. Others probably included Martin Luther, Mother Teresa, Martin Luther King, Jr, . . . . I thought that would be too easy. I decided it would be far more interesting to pick people no one was likely to have heard of, who were not clergy or at least whose contributions were not in areas we normally associate with clergy, and who made contributions in a variety of fields.

1

Chuck loved it. He said it was the most effective way of communicating what worldview is and how it affects all of life that he had seen, and insisted I give it for all the Centurions classes. The next year, I did it again but with different people. When the staff at Breakpoint realized I could extend the series, they suggested I turn them into articles for the website. I did around sixty over the next few years, most of which were lost when they redesigned the website. I had my copies, however, and so I decided it was time to turn them into a book.

Unfortunately, most of the publishers I approached were not interested: they said no one would want a book about people they had never heard of, demonstrating conclusively that their acquisitions editors were missing the point.

When I asked Canon Press if they might be interested in publishing it, they said yes; when I explained the reasoning of the publishers who had turned it down, they shook their heads. They understood far better than the other Christian publishers I had approached the point of the book and why their audience would want to read it.

The result is in your hands.

The biographies are drawn from people living from the fourth to the twentieth century, from Africa, Asia, Europe, and North America, both men and women, active in a wide range of pursuits including evangelism and missions, education, fighting for human rights, government, medicine, and mathematics and science.

The selection shows us that Christianity is not an exclusively Western phenomenon, that from early days the Gospel was penetrating and influencing people and cultures in Africa and Asia along with Europe. The biographies demonstrate that God has been working through his people throughout history to accomplish his purposes and to build his Kingdom.

And, as Chuck Colson said years ago, the stories also illustrate the power of a biblical worldview to transform lives and cultures. In the Kingdom, all that is broken is restored. As we live out the reality of Christ's lordship over every area of life, we too, like so many before us, have the opportunity to work with the Holy Spirit as agents of reconciliation and restoration in our world.

May these stories inspire us to live out the Kingdom in our own lives and our spheres of activity, whatever they may be.

# LATE ANTIQUITY &
# THE EARLY MIDDLE AGES

IN THE NEW TESTAMENT ERA AND FOR THE next two hundred or so years, the Roman Empire was largely at peace. The borders to the north stabilized along the Rhine and the Danube rivers, and although there were ongoing battles with the Persian Empire to the east, most of the empire was prosperous, peaceful, and stable. Christianity was growing within the empire despite sporadic, localized persecutions.

Things changed in the third century. In 235, the Emperor Severus Alexander was assassinated by his own troops. This began a period of instability in the empire that lasted around fifty years. Roman generals vied for the imperial title, with fifty different claimants for the throne during the period. The generals would pull their troops from the borders to march on Rome, leaving the empire vulnerable to barbarian invasions and migrations. The Roman military itself was increasingly made up of Germanic mercenaries. Then in 249, the Plague of Cyprian broke out and ravaged the empire until 264. The period also saw peasant revolts, rampant inflation, and people fleeing their homes and work to escape the chaos.

The period came to an end when Diocletian became emperor. Diocletian changed Rome in fundamental ways, ushering in the period historians call Late Antiquity. He divided the empire into four administrative units, each ruled by a co-emperor, in an attempt to find a stable approach to imperial succession to avoid the civil wars that had racked the empire for the previous half century. As part of this, to overawe people with his glory so that they would not consider revolt, he changed the title of emperor from *princeps*—the first member of the Senate—to *dominus*—lord, with all the divine implications of the term. He instituted elaborate ceremonies around himself, and when the Christians refused to acknowledge him as lord, he began the Great Persecution, the most severe persecution of Christians in the Roman world.

Diocletian also instituted a number of heavy-handed laws to stabilize the empire socially and economically by prohibiting people from moving from their homes or working outside of their father's profession.

Diocletian retired in 305. Shortly thereafter, the various rulers of the different sections of the empire went to war with each other, with Constantine emerging as the victor. Constantine would convert to Christianity and declare religious liberty in the empire, thereby decriminalizing Christianity. (Contrary to what is often claimed, he did not make it the state religion of the empire; that was done later by Theodosius I, who nonetheless continued to allow pagans to worship within Roman territory.)

Constantine divided the empire into two parts. The Eastern, Greek-speaking half was wealthier, more sophisticated, more educated, and the economic and cultural center of the empire. Accordingly, Constantine moved his capital to the ancient city of Byzantium, renaming it New Rome though it rapidly became known as Constantinople, Constantine's City.

The Latin West was poorer and much less important than the Greek East despite having Rome as its capital. It was also subject to more invasions over the next century and a half. The Western emperor became little more than a figurehead in the middle of the fifth century; real power was in the hands of the *magister militum*, the military commander of the Western empire. Finally, in 474, the last emperor in Rome was deposed and not replaced, though Roman governance and administration continued in Constantinople. 474 is thus considered somewhat shortsightedly as the fall of the Roman Empire and the beginning of the Early Middle Ages.

# ST. FRUMENTIUS &
# KING EZANA OF AXUM

(?-C. 383, R. 330-C. 360)

*Fathers of Christianity in Axum*

BECAUSE THE ACTS OF THE APOSTLES tells the story of the spread of Christianity within the Roman Empire, we often forget that the Gospel quickly spread beyond Rome's boundaries. Among the Apostles, Thomas preached in India and Bartholomew and possibly Thaddeus in Armenia (which became the first kingdom to accept Christianity). Rome's great enemy Persia had an active church well before Christianity was legalized in the Roman Empire. Overall, there were more Christians outside the boundaries of the Roman Empire than within it for the first thousand years of the Christian era.

Some of this expansion came through Roman trade and diplomatic contacts outside the Mediterranean basin. The empire had relationships with states in Asia, including the Persian Empire, Arabia, India, and China, and even with Africa, notably with the kingdom of Axum, south of Egypt in modern Eritrea and northern Ethiopia. Axum was a powerful and advanced kingdom that served as a trading nexus between the Roman Empire and India. The kingdom exported ivory, tortoiseshell, gold, and emeralds to these lands, and imported silk and spices.

In about 316 AD, two Greek brothers named Frumentius and Edesius left their home in Tyre in modern-day Lebanon to accompany their uncle on a trading voyage to Axum. They stopped at a port city on the Red Sea. A brawl broke out, and the locals ended up slaughtering everyone on board the ship except the two brothers, who were given to Ella Amida, the king of Axum, as slaves.

The two brothers evidently had received a very good education at home, because they rapidly gained the king's favor and became influential figures at court even at their young age. Shortly before his death, Ella Amida freed them. The king's son and heir Ezana was a minor, so the widowed queen Sofya was named regent. She convinced Frumentius and Edesius to stay in Axum to help her educate her son and prepare him for the throne.

Along with educating the prince, the brothers did their best to encourage the growth of Christianity in Axum. Most Christians in the kingdom were foreign merchants, though there were a small number of native Christians as well. Tradition says that the Apostle Matthew introduced the Gospel to Ethiopia, and the "Ethiopian" (literally "dark-skinned") eunuch converted by Philip may have been from Ethiopia as well, though some scholars think that the Queen Candace whom he served was actually in Nubia (modern Sudan) rather than Axum.

The brothers began their efforts to spread Christianity by encouraging foreign Christian merchants to practice their faith openly. They also engaged in evangelism and made some converts among the Ethiopians.

At about the time Ezana came of age, the brothers left the court. Edesius returned to Tyre, where he was ordained as a priest; he later told the brothers' story to the historian Rufinus, who is our best source for their lives. Frumentius accompanied Edesius as far as Alexandria. He had a burning desire to see Axum converted to Christianity, so he appealed to Athanasius, the patriarch of Alexandria, for missionaries and a bishop for the kingdom. Athanasius decided that Frumentius was the best man for the job, so he consecrated him as bishop in 328 and sent him back south to work on converting the kingdom to Christianity.

When Frumentius returned to Axum, he baptized his former pupil King Ezana as a Christian. With the king's support, Frumentius spread the Gospel throughout Ethiopia and built many churches. He is also credited with translating the New Testament into Ge'ez, the language of Ethiopia. In the process, he also developed a more advanced writing system for the language.

Frumentius's work bore fruit. King Ezana made Christianity the official state religion of Axum, making it the third kingdom to embrace Christianity after Armenia and Rome. Not surprisingly, the church in Axum tied itself closely to the Coptic church in Egypt, looking to the patriarch of Alexandria as their spiritual leader. The people accepted Christianity willingly and were so grateful for Frumentius's work that they called him *Kesate Birhan* (Revealer of Light) and *Abba Salama* (Father of Peace); King Ezana also named him the first *Abune*, the head of the Ethiopian Coptic church.

For his part, King Ezana also worked hard to promote Christianity in his kingdom. One example is found in Axum's coinage. About a century before, Axum had become the first African kingdom to mint coins, probably due to the influence of trade with Rome. At the beginning of Ezana's reign, his coins were decorated with a disk and crescent moon, which were symbols of pagan astrological deities. He replaced these symbols with a Christian cross, making Axum the first African state to use the cross on its coinage. As evidence of Axum's widespread trade connections, Ezana's cross-emblazoned coins have been found as far away as India.

Some of King Ezana's coins also include the legend, "May this please the people." S.C. Munro-Hay comments that this inscription is "a rather attractive peculiarity of Aksumite coinage, giving a feeling of royal concern and responsibility towards the people's wishes and contentment."[1] This may also have been an expression of Ezana's biblically based understanding of a king's responsibilities to his subjects in the sight of God.

1. "Aksum: An African Civilisation of Late Antiquity," *Adis Herald*, November 19, 2018, https://www.addisherald.com/9-4-the-mottoes/.

Frumentius's work as bishop did cause one diplomatic problem for King Ezana. Decades earlier, a dispute arose within the church over whether Jesus was God. On the one side, a presbyter named Arius argued that he was the highest created being, but not God incarnate. He was opposed by Athanasius, the patriarch of Alexandria who had consecrated Frumentius. Athanasius supported the orthodox position, that Jesus was fully God. This conflict became so intense that the Roman Emperor Constantine summoned a church council in the city of Nicaea in 325 to debate this point. The council decided in Athanasius's favor, and Arianism was declared a heresy.

Arianism did not go away, however, even within the empire. About thirty years after the Council of Nicaea, an Arian named Constantius II was emperor of Rome. He was displeased that Axum had an orthodox bishop, and so he sent a letter to King Ezana asking him to replace Frumentius with Theophilus, an Arian, and to send Frumentius to Alexandria to be examined for doctrinal errors. Ezana ignored or rejected the request, however, so Frumentius's position was secure.

Like other kingdoms that were rising in power, Axum engaged in conquests of neighboring states. In the second century AD, Axum had conquered the Himyarite Kingdom in modern Yemen and extended its control through much of the southwestern region of the Arabian Peninsula. King Ezana set his sights on Kush, the kingdom of the Nubians. Kush was already in decline when King Ezana conquered the kingdom in about 350 AD. The King Ezana Stone, found in Meroe, the capital of Kush, bears an inscription in Greek,

Sabaean (the language of Axumite territories in southern Arabia), and Ge'ez describing Ezana's conversion to Christianity and his conquest of Kush.

The efforts of Frumentius and Ezana made Ethiopia the first and for centuries the only independent African kingdom to embrace Christianity. Unfortunately, the rise of Islam cut Axum off from the rest of the Christian world, though the fact that Axum had sheltered Mohammed gave them a certain degree of protection from Muslim conquest.

Christianity remained the primary religion in Ethiopia from Frumentius's day to the present. The Ethiopian church continued to be tied to the Coptic church in Egypt until 1959, when the head of the Ethiopian church was named a patriarch in his own right. Nearly 1700 years after Frumentius and Ezana, the Ethiopian Orthodox church is the largest of the Oriental Orthodox churches, with 40–45 million members. This is a very impressive legacy for a young man who started as a merchant apprentice, became a slave, then a tutor to a prince, before being ordained in the church, and for a young king who converted to Christianity and set himself to building a Christian culture for his kingdom.

Frumentius's story also provides an important lesson that, whatever our circumstances, if we keep our eyes on God and take advantage of the opportunities placed before us, we can and will accomplish his purposes for our lives. Even hardship and injustice can be turned to good—even for our oppressors—if we are open to serving as God calls us to do, working as for the Lord, not men.

# ST. COLUMBANUS (540-615)
## *Irish Missionary to Europe*

THE LATIN WEST WAS POORER AND
much less important to the empire than the Greek East
despite having Rome as its capital. It was also subject to
more invasions. Over time, the Western emperor became little more than a figurehead; real power was in the hands of
the *magister militum*, the military commander of the Western empire. Finally, in 474, the last emperor in Rome was
deposed and not replaced.

This event traditionally marks the beginning of the Early
Middle Ages, which lasted until roughly the year 1000. As the
period began, European civilization was in serious decline. The
climate had gotten colder and wetter, resulting in a shorter growing season and declining population. People moved out of the

cities into the countryside to try to survive, with the effect that many cities shrank, relocated, or disappeared altogether. With de-urbanization, education went into steep decline as well.

A number of so-called barbarian successor states took the Roman Empire's place in Western Europe. The most important of these was the kingdom of the Franks. The Franks started in the modern-day Netherlands and western Germany and from there conquered France, then known as Gaul. The Franks were the first Germanic tribe to convert to orthodox Christianity, but the kingdom and its churches quickly degenerated and grew corrupt. Education was abandoned and little faithful Christianity remained. Some areas even reverted to paganism.

Government and administration changed dramatically during this period. The decline in Roman civil authority left administration in the hands of the Church as the last institution standing. But while the Church tried to maintain Roman governing principles, the Franks and other tribes had radically different ideas of government. Eventually these ideas mixed with Roman and ecclesiastical administrative approaches to produce an uneasy blend that would eventually result in feudalism, a new political system in which a lord gave a grant of land to a vassal (i.e., a subordinate noble) along with the right to govern the territory in return for military service. Except during Charlemagne's time (c. 742-814), governing power was decentralized: responsibility to administer justice and maintain order devolved to local lords and vassals instead of kings.

Ireland was an exception to these trends in many respects. Since its conversion to Christianity under St. Patrick (387–461), Ireland developed a unique culture, with its clan-based social structure integrated with the ecclesiastical hierarchy and monasteries. Because the ancient pagan Druids had been extremely well educated, the Irish believed all religious leaders should be well educated too, and so the Irish monasteries became great centers of learning. Into this world, Columbanus was born in 540. As a young man, he was quite good-looking and attracted the attention of a number of young women. But he was also serious about his faith, so he consulted an older woman about what to do. She replied, "Do you remember Samson? David? Solomon? Women are trouble. Get thee to a monastery!"[2]

So Columbanus withdrew to the monastic life over the objections of his family. He literally had to step over his mother's prostrate body at the threshold to his house when he left for the monastery of Lough Erne. He continued his education there, and then moved on to the monastery at Bangor.

At about the age of forty, Columbanus began hearing a call to leave the monastery and go on a *peregrinatio* (literally, a pilgrimage, but carrying with it the idea of exile from which you would never return to your homeland) to preach the Gospel. His abbot eventually agreed to let him go, and so he set sail to Britain, then across the English Channel to Carnac in Brittany in modern France, where he and his twelve companions began their mission around 585.

Columbanus preached his way across the Frankish kingdom until he came to Burgundy, where he was welcomed

---

2. *The Life of St. Columban by the Monk Jonas*, 8, paraphrased, https://sourcebooks.fordham.edu/basis/columban.asp.

by King Gontram and invited to stay. Columbanus agreed, and selected Annegray, a half-ruined Roman fortress in the Vosges Mountains, to start his first monastery.

Columbanus's fame was such that he was quickly inundated with people from all walks of life who wished to join his community. He had so many people coming to him that he started a second monastery at Luxeuil in 590, then another at Fontaines, all of them governed by a strict rule he produced based on the practice of the monastery at Bangor.

Columbanus's popularity began raising the ire of the local bishops. They resented his influence, the strict rules in his monasteries, his using the Celtic approach for setting the date of Easter rather than the Roman method, and the fact that he refused to submit to their authority. Columbanus defended his views strongly both locally and in letters to the papacy.

When Gontram died, he was succeeded by his son Childebert, who also died and passed the kingdom to his son Thierry. Thierry liked Columbanus, but when Columbanus began criticizing the immorality of the royal court, Thierry turned on him and demanded that he follow local church practices. When he refused, he was arrested.

The guards did not keep a close watch on him, perhaps because they were nervous about arresting a holy man. He soon escaped custody and returned to his monastery. Thierry then arrived with troops determined to send Columbanus and his companions back to Ireland. They were taken down the Loire River to the coast and put on a ship. A storm drove it back to shore, however, and the ship's captain refused to have anything more to do with the brothers, so they once again began traveling through the Frankish territories to Metz, then to Mainz, and then south along the Rhine River.

They made their way to Lake Zurich, where persecution by the pagan population prevented them from settling. They then passed on to Lake Constance, where the local chapel had been converted into a pagan temple complete with idols. The area had evidently not been effectively Christianized under the Roman Empire and had thus reverted back to their old ways when Roman authority collapsed. Gall, one of Columbanus's companions, knew the local language, and so Columbanus had him begin preaching. The local population was converted to Christianity, and Gall stayed there to lead the church. About a century later, a monastery was founded there and named St. Gall in his honor.

In 612, local opposition once again caused Columbanus to move, this time into Italy. Northern Italy was ruled by the Lombards, an Arian tribe. The Arians considered themselves Christians but did not believe Jesus was God; instead, they believed he was the first created being with a status similar to an archangel. The Lombard king Agiluf had converted to orthodox Christianity due to the influence of his orthodox wife Theodelinda. Accordingly, Agiluf welcomed Columbanus and invited him to settle in Lombardy. Columbanus accordingly founded a monastery at Bobbio in 614, where he would live out the last year of his life.

It is difficult to exaggerate the importance of Columbanus's work on the continent. He became the prototype for many other Irish missionaries who preached the Gospel throughout Europe. His own monastery at Luxeuil sent out at least sixty-three known missionaries credited with starting over one hundred other monasteries.

Along with evangelism, however, Columbanus's impact was felt most strongly in the field of education. Like all Irish saints, Columbanus believed very strongly that spiritual leadership and education were inseparable. His monasteries were famous for their *scriptoria* and became major centers of literacy and learning. Many of the surviving manuscripts from continental Europe produced over the next century came from scribes trained at the *scriptoria* at Luxeuil, Corbie, or Bobbio. Without his work, literacy would have all but disappeared in Gaul and we would have even fewer manuscripts from that era than we do today.

Along with copying manuscripts, Columbanus's monasteries also developed some of the most celebrated libraries in medieval Europe. Bobbio was particularly famous for its library, so much so that it was a major inspiration for the library in Umberto Eco's novel, *The Name of the Rose*. It was also a stronghold for orthodoxy in Arian Lombardy. And although it was founded after Columbanus's day, the monastery at St. Gall had one of the largest libraries in Europe, again started by Irish and British monks. Almost unique among medieval libraries, it remains intact today.

Columbanus was not the first Christian leader to have a major impact on education, and he would be far from the last. The biblical worldview teaches that God created all things, and so all things are sacred and worthy of study; it also tells us that all truth is God's truth and can and should be studied as an act of devotion to God. In Christianity, the

mind matters, and so Christians have founded schools wherever they went. A good example of this came a century and
a half after Columbanus's death in the person of Alcuin, a
deacon of the cathedral at York and Charlemagne's minister
of education. We will look at his career in the next chapter.

# ALCUIN OF YORK (C. 735-804)
## Father of Medieval Education

ALTHOUGH COLUMBANUS'S MONAS-
teries had a significant long-term impact on education and
a more limited, local impact on church reform, the overall
Frankish kingdom continued to have problems. It was torn
by a series of civil wars over succession to the throne. The
rivals to the throne gave up so much political power to the
nobles that by the 700s, the monarchy had become little more
than an empty title.

This changed when Pepin the Short became king in 752,
ending the Merovingian dynasty and beginning the Carolingian. He was succeeded by his son Charlemagne in 768.
Charlemagne expanded the borders of the kingdom tremendously: to defend the pope, he conquered the Lombards in

northern Italy; to protect his southern borders from the Muslims in Spain, he took an area in northern Spain that became known as the Spanish March; to stop raids from the Saxons, he conquered them; to protect his eastern border from the South Slavs and the Avars, he took some of their territory as well, a territory that became known as the Eastern March (Ostmark, eventually becoming Austria).

Because of these military successes, Charlemagne became the first person since the fall of Rome to control the majority of continental Europe himself; the only others to do so were Charles V (during the Reformation), Napoleon, and Hitler.

Charlemagne realized that given the size of his kingdom, he needed educated people to administer it. So he decided that he would start an education program, headed by the finest scholar he could find. He decided on someone from outside of his territory, a deacon and teacher in York, England, named Alcuin. The church in York had been founded by Irish missionaries, so not surprisingly it was a major center for education. Alcuin was educated at York by Archbishop Egbert, a student of the Venerable Bede, one of the most important scholars in Northumbria and the author of *The Ecclesiastical History of the English People* (731). When he completed his education, he became a teacher and then the director of the school at York. Among other things, he played a very important role in reviving the late Roman liberal arts in the school. The liberal arts was an educational curriculum that included seven subject divided into two groups. The first, the trivium, were language-based arts that focused on subjective human experience. This included grammar (basic language skills), dialectic (a kind of logic done through discussion and dialogue), and rhetoric (effective communication skills). The second group of subjects was the quadrivium, which included mathematical arts that conveyed objective truth. The subjects in this category were arithmetic, geometry, astronomy, and music (understood as the study of ratios or fractions).

When Charlemagne's call came, Alcuin responded somewhat reluctantly. He joined a group of scholars surrounding Charlemagne, but he quickly emerged as the leading light at court.

One of his first responsibilities was to revamp the palace school, which had been created by Charlemagne's predecessors for the royal family but mostly only taught manners and etiquette. Charlemagne wanted a more academic curriculum, and Alcuin obliged by bringing the liberal arts back to education on the continent. He also taught Charlemagne, his children, and the clergy at the palace chapel.

Alcuin developed close relations with the court, giving the nobles and his students nicknames drawn from the Bible or classical literature. The typical evening entertainment included long theological and philosophical discussions in which Charlemagne himself actively participated.

Although the palace school was particularly important to Charlemagne, he realized it could not supply all the educated administrators he needed. Accordingly, Alcuin helped him set up schools in the cathedrals around the kingdom and in the monasteries that had already been providing what little education that was available prior to Alcuin's reforms. Once again, Alcuin brought the liberal arts into these schools and increased the overall quality of education. These schools would ultimately become the foundation of the later, larger revival of education in the eleventh and twelfth centuries.

To help the kingdom run more smoothly, Alcuin believed in standardization. He not only standardized the curriculum in the schools, but in an era in which all books were hand copied and thus prone to error, he set out to provide standard versions of all texts, including the books used in schools, the liturgy, and monastic rules, among other things.

To do this, Alcuin studied the available copies and selected what he thought to be the best text for the document. He then had scribes prepare a number of master copies that were carefully checked against the original. From there, every copy of the document made within the kingdom had to be made directly from one of the master copies. That way, any copying errors would not be propagated further, and all the copies would be very close to the originals.

To make these copies as easy to read as possible, Alcuin and his successors adapted the Irish uncial letters into a new style of handwriting called Carolingian minuscules. These appeared first at the monasteries of Corbie and Tours, where Alcuin would retire.

The systematic program of copying begun by Alcuin and continued by his immediate successors such as Servatus Lupus (c. 805-c. 862) was critical for the preservation of classical literature. Many of our earliest surviving copies of Latin literature date from the Carolingian period, a fact that led to some confusion in the Italian Renaissance.

Italian Renaissance scholars who were busy searching out ancient literature saw these obviously early texts written in their remarkably elegant handwriting and assumed they couldn't possibly have been produced during the "Dark Ages," and so assumed they had to be authentic Roman documents. They then patterned their own handwriting on Carolingian minuscules, creating a handwriting style known as Italic writing, which in turn is the foundation for our handwriting today.

Alcuin also did a significant amount of writing himself, including letters, poetry, theological treatises, biblical commentaries, and textbooks on grammar, dialectic, and rhetoric. Most interestingly, he also produced a textbook on mathematics, which included fifty-three word problems including a number of river crossing problems that are still used in various forms today.

In addition to his work in education, Alcuin acted as an advisor to Charlemagne. For example, Alcuin convinced Charlemagne to stop forcing pagans to be baptized or face execution, a practice Charlemagne had begun as part of a program to pacify the Saxons. Alcuin argued that faith could not be coerced, so even if you force people into baptism, it wouldn't make them Christians. Even after Alcuin's return to his beloved Northumbria in 790, Charlemagne asked him to return to help him deal with the Adoptionist heresy, which argued that Jesus was simply a human, but when God saw his sinless life, he adopted him as his son, thus making him a deity.

Alcuin's impact was far reaching. Even though the palace school only survived for a few generations, the cathedral schools and especially the monastic schools would live on and would spearhead the revival of education centuries later. The liberal arts curriculum Alcuin set in place would be the foundation for education for well over 500 years and continues to have an effect today. His efforts to standardize texts and writing styles and the work of his team to preserve classical literature would be critically important to the intellectual development of the West for even longer.

But for Alcuin, his work was all about serving God and serving the Church by serving Charlemagne. He saw this as a divine calling, even though much of what he did was not directly related to the Church. And though he did have an important impact ecclesiastically and theologically, it is his work in the "secular" arena of education and cultural transmission that he made his biggest mark in living out his faith and making full use of the gifts God had given him.

# HUNAYN IBN ISHAQ (809-873)
## A Christian in the Islamic World

THERE IS A LOT OF MISINFORMATION about the status of Christians in the Muslim world in the Middle Ages. We frequently hear it treated as a golden age of religious toleration on the one hand, or as a period of extreme oppression on the other. The fact is, both sides contain an element of truth, depending on the time period and region.

Similarly, we often hear that Islam was an advanced, sophisticated civilization, far ahead of the barbaric Christians in areas such as medicine, science, and philosophy. This idea results not only from a caricature of Western Europe in the Middle Ages, but also from a myopic view of the Christian world that ignores Christians in the East. Actually, much of the advanced learning of the Muslim world came to them through Christian sources.

When Arab armies exploded out of the Arabian Peninsula to conquer the Persian Empire and much of the Eastern Roman (a.k.a. the Byzantine) Empire, they came as a largely illiterate tribal people with no experience governing extended territories. Like other conquerors in this situation, they relied on the local peoples to provide administrators and educated professionals to help them run their empire. According to Samuel Hugh Moffett, in the earliest period of the caliphate,

> some respected occupations were for years dominated by Christians and Jews. As late as several generations after Muhammad, Christian and Jewish communities of physicians, musicians, and merchants could be found even in Mecca. The caliph 'Uthman is said to have been so impressed with the Christian poet Abu Zubaid that he asked him to come up and sit in honor next to him. Their superior education made Christians much in demand as administrative secretaries and teachers, as philosophers, architects, scientists, and artists, and some rose to high but extremely vulnerable positions in national and provincial government.[3]

Some even became viziers, high-ranking political advisors to sultans and caliphs. Since Christians also dominated the medical field, they also were frequently appointed personal

3. Samuel Hugh Moffett, *A History of Christianity in Asia*, vol. 1, *Beginnings to 1500* (Maryknoll, NY: Orbis Books, 1998), 338.

physicians to the caliphs. In particular, the Nestorian[4] Bakhtishu family held that post nearly continuously for 250 years.

Not surprisingly, Greek learning passed into the Arabic-
speaking world through Christian scholars, primarily Nestorians. The process began in the middle of the eighth century,
roughly a hundred years after the Muslim conquest of Syria,
with the translation of Greek works into Syriac. From there,
Arab scholars gradually became aware of the Greek texts. The
Latin world had lost touch with most of these, with only a
limited number of Greek texts available in Europe during the
Early Middle Ages.

Hunayn ibn Ishaq was born in al-Hira, Iraq, in 809, when
the region was under the control of the Muslim Caliphate.[5] A Nestorian Christian, he grew up speaking Syriac
and Arabic. As a young man, he went to Baghdad to study
medicine under the famous physician and fellow Nestorian
Yuhanna ibn Masawayh.

Along with practicing medicine, Yuhanna was the director of the Baghdad hospital and had written a number of
medical treatises covering subjects such as ophthalmology,
fevers, dietetics, depression, qualifications for physicians,
and medical aphorisms, brief statements of medical principles. He also held public discussions on medical issues and
was famous for his repartee.

---

4. Nestorians separate the human and divine natures of Christ more
sharply than the Eastern Orthodox, Catholic, and Protestant churches do.
They continue to exist in the Assyrian church of the East.
5. 809 was the year of the death of Caliph Harun al-Rashid, the caliph of
*The Thousand and One Nights*.

Hunayn had a lively curiosity and asked so many questions that the exasperated Yuhanna kicked him out of the school. Hunayn promised himself he would return to Baghdad, but in the meantime he went abroad to learn Greek. When he returned, he was able to recite Homer and Galen in their original languages, which so impressed Yuhanna that he reconciled with Hunayn and the two began to work together.

Hunayn put his language skills to work translating Greek works into Syriac and Arabic. This attracted the attention of Caliph al-Manun, who put him in charge of the *Bayt al Hikmah* (the House of Wisdom), an institution dedicated to translating Greek texts and making them available to Arab scholars. The caliph even sent Hunayn into the Byzantine Empire to obtain works by Aristotle and other authors that were unavailable in the caliphate. Hunayn's work was considered so valuable that al-Manun was reported to have paid him the weight of the books he translated in gold.

Hunayn's translation method was unusual. He translated the books from Greek into Syriac, and his son Ishaq translated them from Syriac into Arabic, with Hunayn checking the translation. Hunayn is credited with translating the works of Hippocrates, Dioscorides, Galen, and Plato's *Republic*, several works by Aristotle, the Old Testament from the Septuagint, along with works on agriculture, chemistry, stones, and religion. His son Ishaq became the principal translator of Aristotle into Arabic.

Along with his translations, Hunayn composed original works dealing with philosophy, religion, and medicine. His contributions to ophthalmology were particularly important.

His *Ten Treatises on Ophthalmology* discusses the anatomy of the eye in surprising detail and describes diseases of the eye and their treatments, including surgical remedies for corneal ulcers and therapy for cataracts.

Hunayn developed a close relationship with the Caliph al-Mutawakkil. Recognizing Hunayn's skills as a scholar and translator, the caliph appointed him as his personal physician instead of a member of the Bakhtishu family. A rift developed between al-Mutawakkil and Hunayn, however, when the caliph asked Hunayn to make a poison to kill one of his enemies. Despite offers of generous payment, Hunayn kept putting the caliph off, saying it would take time to prepare such a poison. In the end, the caliph got angry and had Hunayn thrown in prison for a year.

Hunayn was then brought before the caliph and threatened with death, to which he replied, "I have skill only in what is beneficial, and have studied nothing else." The caliph, claiming that he was only testing Hunayn's personal integrity, asked him what kept him from complying with the order. Hunayn responded, "Two things: my religion and my profession. My religion decrees that we should do good even to our enemies, how much more to our friends. And my profession is instituted for the benefit of humanity and limited to their relief and cure. Besides, every physician is under oath never to give anyone a deadly medicine."[6]

Hunayn was therefore released.

6. Moffett, *A History of Christianity in Asia*, vol. 1, 355.

Despite his support for translation, al-Mutawakkil was concerned about foreign ideas influencing Islam and about Muslim scholars who advocated a less literal interpretation of the Quran. As a result, he enforced a rigid Sunni orthodoxy on the state and began persecuting more liberal Muslim thinkers as well as increasing the pressure on Christians in the caliphate. This would be a harbinger of things to come both in the Muslim world and for the Christians in the Middle East.

After al-Mutawakkil was murdered by one of his sons, Hunayn enjoyed the support of his successors and continued his work of translation until his death.

As we can see from the life of Hunayn, Christians played important roles in government and scholarship in the Muslim world. That is not to say, however, that they were generally treated well. There were periodic outbreaks of violent persecution, including widespread destruction of churches, and they were clearly second-class citizens subject to ever-increasing oppression as the decades moved forward. Al-Mutawakkil's caliphate marked the beginning of the slow decline of Christianity in the Muslim world from a combination of persecution and external pressures, the loss of the missionary zeal that drove the Nestorians in earlier centuries, and internal decay within the churches.

Nonetheless, it is an important if largely unrecognized fact that Nestorian Christians played a far more central role in developing the medieval Muslim intellectual and medical tradition. Western Europe would eventually benefit from this, as works of Aristotle translated by Hunayn and his son would pass to scholars from the Latin world via Islamic Spain.

Ironically enough, in the long run, the Latins would make far more extensive use of Aristotle than the Muslims. Medieval European philosophy, theology, science, and political theory would advance tremendously because of the "New Aristotle" coming from Spain. Al-Mutawakkil's distrust of foreign ideas would become increasingly the norm in the Muslim world, and so speculative learning from foreign sources would be banned while practical learning (e.g., medicine) would be embraced as long as it did not contradict the Quran.

Hunayn himself played the role of a Daniel in many ways, serving in the court of non-Christian rulers who were at times openly hostile to his faith. His scholarship, medical skills, and personal integrity born of his faith enabled him to survive and serve there, leaving an enormous and wideranging legacy in his own era and beyond. For those in positions of influence in cultural or political situations opposed to the Gospel, Hunayn provides a model of how to live: Do your work to the best of your ability, live with integrity, and whatever ups or downs might follow, never compromise your obedience and faithfulness to God.

# LEIF ERIKSON (C. 970-C. 1020)
## Viking and Explorer of America

WHEN WE THINK ABOUT VIKINGS, the two things that most often come to mind are longboats full of warriors raiding and pillaging the countryside, and their desire to die in battle so they could enter Valhalla to serve as warriors for Odin in the battle of Ragnarok at the end of the world.[7] In popular culture today, the most famous Viking is probably the legendary but historically questionable Ragnar Lothbrok. However, the best-known fully historical

7. Norse religion believed that at the end of the world—Ragnarok—the gods would battle the frost giants and other monsters, and all would be destroyed except for a few humans and gods who would start the world anew. Odin, the chief of the gods, brought warriors who died in battle to his palace of Valhalla where they would prepare to take their place in the war at the end of the world.

Vikings are probably Erik the Red, the founder of the first Viking settlement in Greenland, and his son Leif Erikson, the first known European to make it to North America.

Despite our image of the Vikings as heathens, worshippers of the old Norse gods, by the tenth century many Vikings were Christians, including Leif Erikson. In fact, his trip to North America was part of a missionary effort to reach the Viking settlements in Greenland.

The Norse languages did not have a word for religion; the existence of gods and spirits was simply assumed. As a result, Christianity, a monotheistic religion with systematic organization and doctrine, was completely foreign to them. Further, the Vikings respected prowess in battle, and so they held Christians and especially clergy in contempt since they were utterly unable to defend themselves against attack. Only when Christian kings and bishops began leading military forces successfully against them did the Vikings began taking Christianity seriously.

Initially, Vikings were forcibly converted to Christianity: after losing a battle, the leaders were forced to accept baptism in hopes that it would make them less warlike. It didn't always work: one Danish *jarl* in England who "converted" with his overlord complained that his baptismal robe was much less fine than the ones he wore all the other times he had been baptized.

Sometimes conversion did stick to varying degrees. Rollo the Viking, for example, adopted Christianity to acquire the duchy of Normandy from King Charles the Simple of France. Rollo used Christianity to consolidate his control over the region. On his death he gave one hundred pounds of gold to Christian churches, but also hung one hundred prisoners as a sacrifice to Odin. Similarly, many Viking graves included both crosses and Thor's hammers, suggesting either syncretism or that the Vikings were hedging their bets.

Others, though, took Christianity much more seriously, perhaps too seriously. Olaf Tryggvason, the son of Tryggvi Olafson and king of Norway, accepted Christianity and attempted to convert people by force, including torturing people and executing those who refused to become Christians. One of those who converted willingly was Leif Erikson.

Leif came from a colorful family. His grandfather Thorvald had been banished from Norway for killing several people, so he sailed west and settled in Iceland. Some years later, Thorvald's son Erik the Red got into a feud with some of his neighbors and killed them. He was exiled from Iceland for three years, but during this time he got into another conflict and killed several other local Vikings, so he was declared an outlaw for three more years. As a result, Erik sailed west to establish the first Viking settlement in Greenland. His son Leif was born there.

Leif was raised by one of Erik's thralls (i.e., slaves) named Tyrker, whom Leif considered to be his foster father. In 999 Leif traveled to Norway, where he became part of Olaf Tryggvason's retinue. Leif converted to Christianity, and then was sent to introduce the religion to Greenland.

We don't often appreciate the difficulties the Vikings faced sailing west across the Atlantic. Their ships had square sails, which means they could not tack into the wind; the wind had to be blowing from behind them for the sails to propel the ship. Since the prevailing winds in the north Atlantic blow from west to east, to sail west, the Vikings had to rely on storms. Severe storms turn cyclonic, that is, the winds circulate counterclockwise around the eye. This means that by riding the north edge of the storms, the Vikings could take advantage of westward blowing winds to propel them across the ocean.

Not surprisingly perhaps, Vikings were sometimes blown off course. This had happened to a Viking merchant Leif had met who claimed to have seen land west of Greenland. Leif himself was blown off course trying to reach Greenland; he spotted the land and picked up two shipwrecked sailors there. He seems to have explored the territory a bit before returning to Greenland.

The following year, he returned to North America, which he named Vinland ("wine land") because of the abundance of grapes he found there. He explored the region, established a small settlement where he wintered, and returned to Greenland with a cargo of timber and grapes. Vikings would later return and establish other settlements, none of which lasted long, though for centuries the descendants of the Vikings returned periodically to harvest timber and possibly to trade.

After his stay on Vinland, Leif returned to Greenland to fulfill his mission to bring Christianity to the country. His mother Tjodhilde quickly converted, though Erik the Red adamantly refused. (His mother then refused to sleep with him, much to Erik's annoyance, according to the sagas. Some sources say he eventually converted as a result.) Tjodhilde is credited with building the first church in North America.

Leif settled in Greenland and succeeded in his mission of converting Viking Greenland from paganism to Christianity. The region remained firmly Christian for the rest of its history. The last document from Norse Greenland is an account of a wedding held at Hvalsey Church in 1408, just before the territory was abandoned.

# GUDRID
# THORBJARNARDÓTTIR

## (C. 980-C. 1019)

### *"The Far Traveler"*

THE PREVIOUS CHAPTER ON LEIF Erikson pointed out that there were Christian Vikings. In this chapter we will look at the remarkable career of another Norse Christian, Gudrid Thorbjarnardóttir, known in her native Iceland as Gudrid the Far Traveler.

As her name indicates, Gudrid was the daughter of Thorbjorn, a Viking chieftain in Iceland. A man named Einar proposed to Gudrid, but Thorbjorn refused on the grounds that Einar's father was a slave; instead, Gudrid married Thorir, a Norwegian merchant. The family left Iceland for Greenland with Erik the Red, but bad weather delayed their arrival until winter. According to the *Saga of the Greenlanders,* Leif Erikson rescued Gudrid and fifteen men and brought them to Brattahlid, Erik the Red's colony. Thorir died of illness that winter, leaving Gudrid a widow.

One winter in Greenland during a period of dearth, Gudrid was invited to the home of a chieftain named Thorkel. A seeress named Thorbjorg came to prophesy, but she needed women to sing a "weird-song" (i.e., a magical enchantment). Gudrid admitted to having been taught the weird-songs by her foster mother Halldis, but she refused to do so because she was a Christian. Thorbjorg and Thorkel pressured her to sing, and she gave in and sang the weird-song with an exceptionally beautiful voice according to the *Saga of Erik the Red.*

Some sources attempt to date Gudrid's conversion to much later in her life after she returned to Iceland. This story shows that she came to her Christian faith early in life, probably in her childhood. Christian missionaries had arrived in Iceland in 980, about the year of her birth. They made only slow progress at first, though after Olaf Tryggvason, a native of Iceland, became king of Norway, he put increasing pressure on the Icelanders to convert, including banning trade with Iceland until they became Christians, taking hostages and threatening to kill them, and the like. In 1000, Christianity was made the official religion in Iceland.

Gudrid was well-liked by Erik the Red and the people of Brattahlid. She was courted by and married Leif Erikson's younger brother Thorstein Erikson. According to the *Saga of the Greenlanders,* she accompanied him on a voyage to Vinland (North America) to try to recover the body of his brother

Thorvald; according to the *Saga of Erik the Red*, however, they only married after Thorstein had completed that voyage alone. One way or another, the two spent the winter at Lysufjord, a Viking settlement on the west coast of Greenland. Illness struck, however, and Thorstein died. According to the sagas, he prophesied about Gudrid's future on his deathbed, with the *Saga of the Greenlanders* putting particular focus on Christianity as part of that prophecy. Shortly thereafter her father Thorbjorn also died, leaving everything to Gudrid.

Gudrid returned to Brattahlid, where Erik the Red encouraged a wealthy Icelandic merchant named Thorfinn Karlsefni to marry her. After their marriage, at Gudrid's urging, he set off with sixty men, five women, and a cargo of livestock to establish a settlement on Vinland, having gotten Leif Erikson's permission to use buildings he had put up on his earlier expedition there. That autumn, somewhere between the years 1004 and 1013, Gudrid bore him a son named Snorri Thorfinnson, the first known European born in North America.

The Vinland colony lasted about three years. Some scholars believe that during this time they explored as far south as Manhattan. Ultimately, though, conflicts with the native peoples, whom they called *Skraelingar* ("barbarians") led them to abandon the colony and return to Greenland.

Karlsefni and Gudrid then made their way to Iceland, possibly after going to Norway. The couple settled at Karlsefni's family estate where they had other children. Karlsefni's mother was initially contemptuous of Gudrid, though she soon realized that "she was a lady without peer" and accepted the marriage. After Karlsefni died, Gudrid took over running the estate until Snorri married, at which point she passed control of the estate to him.

Gudrid was not done with her travels, however. *The Saga of the Greenlanders* tell us she traveled south; according to some stories, she went on a pilgrimage to Rome, where she met the pope and gave him a report on the state of the church in Iceland and Greenland. She then returned home to Snorri in Iceland.

Snorri, meanwhile, played an important role in Icelandic Christianity: one of his grandsons and two of his great-grandsons would become bishops. He built a church near his estate where Gudrid took up residence and lived the rest of her life as a nun and anchoress (i.e., a hermit). We have no clear date for her death, but it was probably around 1019.

Assuming the dates we have for her life are accurate, she was about thirty-nine years old.

Gudrid's life was full of adventure, but she also faced many hardships, including the deaths of her husbands, traveling across the north Atlantic in longships, which is difficult and dangerous even today, and being part of a settlement in unknown territory with hostile local people. Through it all, her faith was a central feature of her life as demonstrated by her descendants' roles in Icelandic Christianity, by her pilgrimage to Rome, and by her decision to withdraw from society and live as a hermit—an act of deep piety in her time and culture. Rather than continue her adventures, she was content to dedicate her life to prayer and service of God, which speaks volumes about her desires and priorities.

# THE CENTRAL MIDDLE AGES

ALTHOUGH WE OFTEN HEAR THE Middle Ages called the Dark Ages, that term is only used by British historians to describe the Early Middle Ages as a period for which we do not have many records—it is historically dark in the sense that we cannot see into it. The Central Middle Ages, beginning around the year 1000, are a different matter altogether.

By the turn of the millennium the climate in Europe grew warmer and drier, making for a longer growing season. This led to a chain of effects: crops were easier to grow, leading to better nutrition and longer lifespans. Because it was easier to set up your own household, people married younger, leading to more births; as a result, population more than doubled between the years 1000 and 1300. Surplus population in the countryside led to the growth of cities, the expansion of trade and manufacturing, and a virtual industrial revolution in the period.

The growth in cities paralleled a centralization of power in the Holy Roman Empire (roughly modern Germany and Austria) and in the kingdoms of France and England. Church reform movements led to a revival of the papacy. All of this in turn led to an explosion in education and especially legal studies, as both ecclesiastical and civil governments needed educated people to work in their bureaucracies. This led to the rise of scholasticism, the flourishing of theological studies, and even important developments in natural philosophy and theology.[8]

We also see remarkable developments in architecture and an artistic style that emphasized realistic portrayals of the world well before parallel developments in the Italian Renaissance. Vernacular and Latin literature, new musical styles and notation, and a host of other innovations mark the period.

In short, the Middle Ages were anything but dark.

---

8. Natural philosophy and natural theology both study the natural world but look at it in terms of its philosophical and theological implications. The natural sciences of today are related but reduced versions of natural philosophy and natural theology: they do no more than aim at knowledge of the physical world as an end in itself without regard for anything beyond the phenomena.

# HILDEGARD VON BINGEN

(1098-1179)

*Polymath and Mystic*

THE CATHOLIC CHURCH IN THE Middle Ages did not allow women much opportunity for public ministry. The only role available to women in the Church was as nuns in closed monastic communities. Although the abbesses that ran these monasteries could have a fair amount of political clout, their role as spiritual leaders was limited to their convent, and even then was exercised under the direction of a male priest. Although the secular world would become more and more open over the next centuries to women playing a role in public life, the Church did not follow suit.

The sole exception to the exclusion of women from leadership roles in the church was female mystics, women who received a direct experience of God that transcended reason. Many Christians today look with suspicion on mysticism, and for good reason. People claiming to be mystics have promoted some frankly flaky or outright heretical ideas. And yet at its root, mysticism simply involves a sense of being in God's presence, connecting us in our daily life with transcendental reality. This may involve some sort of peak emotional experience, or it may be simply "the practice of the presence of God" as seventeenth-century monk Brother Lawrence put it in his book by that name. Mysticism involves an inner religious experience that is more than simply rational. Although we usually associate it with Catholicism or Eastern Orthodoxy, it was part of the Protestant reformer's religious life. For Luther it was found in music; Calvin explained that there was more going on in his experience of the Eucharist than he could put in words. This inability to express a religious experience is one of the hallmarks of mysticism.

If authenticated by the Church, a mystic gained a great deal of influence since he or she had a kind of immediate relationship with God that went well beyond the experience of the church hierarchy. The Middle Ages saw many women mystics, most of whom had only a local following. The greatest mystic of the twelfth century, Hildegard von Bingen, was well known across Europe and had an influence far beyond any other woman in the Church of her time.

Hildegard was the tenth child of a noble family. She started getting visions at about the age of three and realized what they were when she was five. Perhaps because of the visions or perhaps as a way of improving their political position, her parents Hildebert and Mechthilde gave her to a monastery to be raised as a nun at age eight.

Hildegard spent her first years in the monastery essentially as an apprentice to a nun named Jutta. Jutta was a visionary herself and attracted followers who visited her in the convent. When she died in 1136, Hildegard was unanimously elected *magistra* ("master," or teacher) at the convent. At about the same time, the local abbot asked Hildegard to become prioress of the convent, which would have placed her under his authority. If she was going to run the convent, however, she wanted more independence, and so she went over the abbot's head to the archbishop, who granted her the right to start her own convent at Rupertsberg. She only made the move in 1150, fourteen years after Jutta's death. She later founded another monastery at Eibingen.

In 1541, while she was fighting to get her own monastery, Hildegard received a vision in which God told her to "write down that which you see and hear." Prior to this, she had only confided her visions to Jutta, who then told their confessor, a priest named Volmar, about them. Hildegard resisted following these instructions, but she got very sick as a result of her disobedience (as she interpreted it). She got better when she began to dictate the visions to Volmar, and over the next ten years she produced her first theological treatise, *Scivias* ("Know the ways"). This was followed by two more, *Liber vitae meritorum* ("The book of life's merits") and *Liber divinorum operum* ("The book of divine work"), the last of which she completed at age seventy-five. Each of these volumes consists of a description of her visions, then an interpretation of them drawn from Scripture. She also either painted or supervised the painting of some of these visions.

Hildegard's writings were submitted to the bishop, who pronounced them as coming from God. They were then brought to the attention of Pope Eugenius III, who also approved them. As a result people began to write and visit Hildegard looking for help with physical healing and for spiritual advice.

Perhaps for this reason, or perhaps because all of her life she had been weak and sickly, Hildegard developed expertise in medicine. She believed that Genesis taught that all things were made for the good of humanity, so she thought that herbs, water, animals, and precious stones all had healing properties. She wrote about these in another book, *Causae et curae* ("Causes and cures") and produced a book on natural theology entitled *Physica*.

As a recognized visionary, Hildegard earned the right to be heard in circles that otherwise would have paid no attention to an abbess of a small convent in the woods of Germany. She corresponded with four popes, one king, Holy Roman Emperor Frederick Barbarossa (who invited her to meet with him personally), St. Bernard of Clairvaux, ten archbishops, nine bishops, forty-nine abbots (including the famous Abbot Suger from St. Denis outside of Paris, one of the most important clerics of his day), twenty-three abbesses, and many more members of the lower clergy. And that's only in one manuscript of her writings; there are more letters in a second manuscript. Each of these either sought her advice or listened very carefully to her counsel when it came unsolicited. Altogether, nearly 400 of her letters survive.

In an era when very few priests preached, and women never did aside from abbesses and prioresses within their own convents, Hildegard was invited to do four separate preaching tours. She preached publicly, to both lay and clerical audiences, and focused on clerical abuses and Church reform.

While doing all of this, she was also running her monastery and seeing to the spiritual life of her nuns. She wrote one of the earliest surviving morality plays, *Ordo virtutum* ("Play of the virtues") for them. Most famously, she produced an impressive body of liturgical music, which is collected in a cycle entitled *Symphonia armoniae celestium revelationum*. Altogether, we have sixty-nine of her songs (words and music), and the words for four more, making her one of the most prolific known composers of the period. These use soaring monophonic melodies (i.e., there is one line only, with no harmony) that break the mold of the liturgical music of the period. Among other things, the melodies are connected very closely to the emotions of the words, something that traditional chant did not do. Hildegard's music is considered some of the finest produced in the Middle Ages.

After her death, Hildegard was one of the first people to go through the formal process of canonization by the Catholic church, though perhaps because the process was so new it got bogged down and the process was not completed. Recently, the church hierarchy has restarted the procedure and is scheduled to declare her a saint and a Doctor of the Church (i.e., a teaching theologian) in October 2012.

Even without canonization, however, Hildegard is a remarkable example of a woman who overcame tremendous physical challenges and the constraints placed upon her by her culture to accomplish great things and to influence her time for the Gospel. She took full advantage of all the gifts and opportunities God provided her, and had a tremendous impact in theology, politics, medicine, art, music, and Church reform, as well as in the lives of the individuals she touched. That we can see the artwork and hear the music inspired by her visions today further extends her influence to our day and continues to bless people over eight centuries after her death.

Hildegard was also a harbinger of things to come, at least in the secular realm. Over time, women began to play a much larger role in society than our stereotypes would suggest. They ran businesses, bought and sold property, and went on pilgrimage without male minders as shown by Chaucer's wife of Bath in the *Canterbury Tales*. The fifteenth-century French woman Christine de Pizan is the first known person to make a living purely as an author. The medieval period had its misogynistic points, especially with respect to the clergy, but women nonetheless were much more influential and active in society than we usually recognize.

# ROBERT GROSSETESTE

## (C. 1170–1253)

*Theologian and Scientist*

THE MIDDLE AGES ARE GENERALLY thought of as being a period shot through with superstition and ignorance, and while there is some truth in this especially on a popular level, medieval scholars were active in what we today call science. "Medieval science" may sound like an oxymoron, but the Middle Ages saw a number of important advancements in science that laid the foundation for the discoveries of the Scientific Revolution.

Much of the foundation for this was laid by a shift in worldview in the cathedral schools of the twelfth century. Known as "Platonic humanism," this worldview argued that since the world came from God, studying the world can lead us back to

God. In other words, understanding the world as God made it reveals the mind of God and is thus a theological activity.

One of the key figures in the early phases of medieval scientific advancement was the unfortunately named Robert Grosseteste. (His last name can be translated "fat head.") Grosseteste came from a humble background to rise to be an important church statesman, theologian, educator, and eventually bishop of Lincoln, where he is buried.

We know surprisingly little with any degree of certainty about Grosseteste's education and early career. He was educated in a cathedral school, possibly at Hereford. He showed such ability in the liberal arts, canon law, and even medicine that in 1192, Gerard of Wales recommended him for a position to William de Vere, bishop of Hereford. Grosseteste worked for de Vere until the latter's death in 1198, after which Grosseteste disappears from the historical record for a while.

In 1225, he was given a benefice in the diocese of Lincoln, and in 1229 became an archdeacon at Leicester and a canon of the cathedral at Lincoln, the largest diocese in England. (Canons were the priests who elected the bishop.) After a serious illness in 1232, which he thought was divine judgment for holding multiple offices, he resigned from his benefice and as archdeacon, keeping only his office as canon.

In 1229, he also began teaching theology at the Franciscan convent in the relatively new University of Oxford, which was in the diocese of Lincoln. His teaching would have a major influence on Franciscan theology for the next century.

In 1235, when Bishop Hugh de Wells of Lincoln died, the canons split over who should be the next bishop. Grosseteste was elected as a compromise candidate and spent the next eighteen years until his death as the bishop of Lincoln.

Once elected bishop, Grosseteste became heavily involved in ecclesiastical politics. He was very concerned about church leadership and problems of corruption in the clergy. Among other things, he got into a conflict with the Archbishop of Canterbury, Boniface of Savoy. This conflict brought Grosseteste before Pope Innocent IV in 1250, where at the age of eighty he lectured Innocent about the problems in the church and laid the blame squarely at the feet of the papacy.

For our purposes, however, it is his work as a theologian and educator that is Grosseteste's most important contribution to the Church. He continued his scholarly work at the university and oversaw its teaching even while involved in his reform program. His theological treatises and teaching shaped Franciscan thought as well as laying the foundation for theology at Oxford more generally. His work on ecclesiology would be a major influence on the English reformer John Wyclif a century after Grosseteste's death.

Along with producing a number of important theological treatises, Grosseteste also learned Greek and translated the theology of John of Damascus and the entire corpus of Pseudo-Dionysius (a major influence on medieval mysticism) into Latin.

In addition to his work on formal theology and his translations, Grosseteste had a major impact on the development of medieval science, both in terms of methodology and content.

Grosseteste was one of the first medieval thinkers to understand Aristotle's approach to studying the natural world, an approach that he called "resolution and composition." This was an early version of the scientific method. It begins with observation of particulars, which leads to the formulation of a universal law that governs the particulars ("resolution"). This law is then used to make predictions about other particulars ("composition"). Both resolution and composition need to be verified through experimentation and additional observation, not through pure logic.

Grosseteste's methodology would continue to shape natural philosophy (i.e., studies of the natural world) into the seventeenth century and the beginnings of the scientific revolution, including influencing Galileo.

Another important element of Grosseteste's thought was the idea that sciences followed a hierarchical order. For example, optics depends on geometry; this means that geometry is foundational for optics and thus that optics is subordinate to geometry.

More generally, Grosseteste followed the late Roman writer Boethius in arguing that since the natural sciences are based on mathematics, mathematics is the highest of the sciences. Although the role of mathematics in the sciences is widely understood today, Grosseteste's rediscovery of that truth made it a principle in medieval natural philosophy that then carried over to the founders of modern science.

In the realm of natural science, Grosseteste was particularly interested in optics, a fascination that he also passed on to the next generation of Franciscan theologians. Of all the topics included in natural philosophy, optics was seen as being particularly important because it had the closest connection to epistemology, the branch of philosophy that deals with knowledge.

Following St. Augustine of Hippo, Grosseteste argued that the only way we can know truth is through illumination. He used the workings of physical light to explain this: just as we cannot see a body unless it has light shining on it, so the mind cannot comprehend truth unless divine light illuminates it. This divine light is none other than the *logos*, Jesus, the Light of the World. All knowledge of truth, for Christian and non-Christian alike, is mediated by Christ through the process of divine illumination.

For Grosseteste, understanding light had much greater significance even than its application to epistemology. Grosseteste believed that Genesis 1 taught that light was the first element of creation, and thus that light was the basis from which everything else was made. In fact, light was at the foundation of Grosseteste's entire cosmology, as well as his understanding of the relationship between soul and body.

Along with his use of light throughout his speculative philosophy, Grosseteste also studied it as a physical phenomenon. He worked with spherical glass bowls filled with water, lenses, and other tools to explore the behavior of light, and made significant advances in optics that would lead over the next years to the development of eyeglasses, among other things. Some scholars today even suggest that he had a very modern understanding of how color works centuries before Isaac Newton would demonstrate the visible spectrum in white light.

Grosseteste's work married philosophical and theological reflection, mysticism, and observation and experimentation in the natural realm to produce a highly integrated vision of the world that is foreign to the way we think today. Our worldview tends to be fragmented: we rarely if ever try to connect discoveries in science with ethics or philosophy; our beliefs in the nature of reality do not connect to our understanding of knowledge or psychology; we do not attempt to connect beauty, say in the arts, with our theology. Yet for Grosseteste and other medieval thinkers, everything was integrated under theology as the queen of the sciences. His groundbreaking work in scientific methodology, in mathematizing natural philosophy, and the specific conclusions he reached with regard to optics were important advancements in knowledge in the Middle Ages that had a profound influence on his students and on theology and natural philosophy for the next several centuries, putting the lie to the entire notion of the "Dark Ages."

# GEBRE MESQEL LALIBELA

## (R. 1181-1221)

### *Christian King of Axum*

WE OFTEN THINK OF CHRISTIANITY as a European phenomenon, but as we saw in the previous chapter on St. Frumentius and King Ezana, the first kingdom to convert to Christianity was Armenia and the third was Axum in modern Ethiopia. The Axumite kingdom continued as a Christian kingdom, though Muslim expansion into Egypt cut it off from its patriarchate in Alexandria and from the Latin West and the Byzantine Empire.

The Axumite kingdom came to an end when Gudit or Yodit (Judith) overthrew the king, attempted to exterminate the royal family, and set herself up as queen in 960. Little is known about her, though she might have been part of the *Beta Israel*, native Ethiopian Jews who date back to the period before Ezra. Alternately, she may have been a pagan. One way or another, she was no friend of Christianity: she destroyed churches and monuments and seems to have been bent on ending Christianity in the area.

Gudit's successors ruled Ethiopia until they were overthrown in 1137 by Mara Takla Haymanot, the founder of the Zagwe dynasty. To solidify his claim to the throne, Mara married a member of the royal family of Axum. The Zagwe dynasty also returned the kingdom to its 800-year-old Christian tradition, and despite considerable pressure from Islam, Ethiopia has remained a largely Christian country to this day.

The most famous member of the Zagwe dynasty was Gebre Mesqel Lalibela. Lalibela was born in Roha, the Zagwe capital, which was later renamed Lalibela after him. Legend says a swarm of bees surrounded him at his birth and landed on him without stinging him, and so he was named Lalibela, which means "bees obey him." His mother took this as a prophecy that he would become emperor of Ethiopia. Not surprisingly, this did not make him popular with other members of his family. The king and his brother, one of Lalibela's uncles, sent him into exile, and he was nearly poisoned by his half-sister.

As a young man, Lalibela claimed to have had visions and spent some time as a hermit. In 1180, he made a pilgrimage to Jerusalem, which was then in the hands of the Crusaders. During this period, Lalibela's half-brother Harba was on the throne. The Ethiopian clergy were unhappy with him because of his diplomatic contacts with the papacy. Evidently, they feared Roman interference into their church's affairs. When Lalibela returned from his pilgrimage in 1181, the clergy urged him to take the throne from Harba. He reluctantly agreed, and so he became king of Ethiopia.

Lalibela took the name Gebre Mesqel (Servant of the Cross) and began his reign with an extended fast. He attempted to rule as a Christian monarch, emphasizing peace and charity. He worked to secure his borders and to maintain good relations with Saladin, the premier leader in the Muslim world. He wanted to protect Ethiopian Christians in Muslim territories, and his positive relations with Saladin helped secure their safety.

On the other hand, Lalibela was on the throne in 1187 when Saladin destroyed the armies of the Crusader states at the Horns of Hattin and then conquered Jerusalem. Lalibela was concerned that the fall of the city would make pilgrimage increasingly difficult for his people.

Lalibela decided that he needed to recreate the city of Jerusalem in his capital city. The city's river was renamed the Jordan, and a number of other locations were given biblical names. Most importantly, however, Lalibela commissioned the building of a network of rock-hewn churches connected by an intricate system of tunnels that were intended to be a symbolic representation of Jerusalem.

There are a total of eleven rock-hewn churches in Roha/ Lalibela. These are all monolithic churches, meaning that they are carved from a single rock rather than built of stone masonry. The craftsmen carved a wide trench in the bedrock around the four sides of the churches, and then went to work with hammers and chisels to carve out the church building itself, including doors, windows, moldings, crosses, etc. The roofs are level with the ground, and the entrances are reached by staircases down to the level of the excavated courtyard.

Each church is unique, though they follow the design of Axumite churches. The northern group includes the largest monolithic church in the world, Bete Adhane Alem (House of the Savior of the World). This church is believed to be a copy of the Cathedral of St. Mary of Mt. Zion in Axum, where the Ethiopian church believes the biblical Ark of the Covenant is housed.

Bete Adhane Alem is linked by tunnels and walkways to Bete Maryam (House of St. Mary), which may be the oldest of the churches. A line of geometrically carved windows in the east wall of Bete Maryam illuminates the church's copy of the Ark of the Covenant. The church also includes a number of painted decorations. Also in the northern group is Bete Golgotha, which includes life-size carvings of saints and the tomb of Emperor Lalibela. The Selassie Chapel and the Tomb of Adam complete the northern set of churches.

Several churches in the eastern group may be older than the other churches, at least in origin. There is some speculation that some of them predate Lalibela by 500 years and had been used earlier on as government buildings. This set includes Bete Amanuel, which may have been a royal chapel; Bete Merkorios, which may have originated as a prison; Bete Gabriel-Rufael, possibly a former royal palace; and Bete Abba Libanos, a church built by Lalibela's widow in his honor.

The best preserved and most spectacular of the churches is Bete Giyorgis (House of St. George). Located to the west, this was probably the last church completed. It stands forty feet high, making it the tallest of the churches, and is in the shape of a Greek cross.

In addition to the churches in Roha/Lalibela proper, twelve miles away is the eleventh-century Yemrehanna Kristos church, built in the style of Axumite churches but constructed in a cave.

As if the churches themselves were not impressive enough, Lalibela also built wells at many of the churches, fed by artesian springs that bring water up to the ridge on which the city is built. This feat of engineering makes Hezekiah's tunnel in old Jerusalem look like child's play in comparison.

The monolithic churches at Roha/Lalibela are so amazing that a variety of legends have grown up around them. One popular legend says that angels worked on them at night when the workers went home. Bete Maryam contains a pillar on which it is said Lalibela carved the secrets of the churches' construction, though the pillar is kept covered and so no one really knows what is on it except perhaps the monks at the church. Some people have suggested that the Knights Templar were involved in their construction, but there is no evidence that they were, and the Ethiopian designs of the buildings effectively refute that claim. Records do indicate that foreign workers were involved in their construction, but given the artistic work they were most likely Copts from Egypt.

Lalibela's reign after he began building the churches was not very smooth, though the scarcity of primary sources makes it difficult to get clear information about his years as king. The official version of events states that his principal wife convinced him to abdicate in favor of his nephew Na'akueto La'ab, the son of Harba whom Lalibela had deposed. After eighteen months, however, some of Na'akueto La'ab's soldiers took a poor farmer's only cow for the king's dinner table; this kind of abusive behavior led Lalibela to take back the throne, again at the urging of his wife, and give it to his own son Yetbarak. This story may mask intrigue and dissatisfaction with Lalibela's rule that led Na'aketo La'ab to stage a coup; he in turn was overthrown by Yetbarak. Alternately, it could represent the two of them jockeying for power in the waning years of Lalibela's life.

Either way, Lalibela was revered as a saint and after his death was canonized by the Ethiopian Orthodox church. Roha was renamed after him, and his churches became the second most important pilgrimage destination in Ethiopia after Axum and a UNESCO World Heritage Site. When we think of Christian architecture, we often think of the Gothic cathedrals of medieval Europe, which were built at roughly the same time as Lalibela's rock-hewn churches. Both illustrate in different ways that the architects and artisans of the period developed new and innovative technologies to achieve their vision of what a Christian church should be. The beauty and genius of the medieval buildings inspire awe and lead directly to contemplation of God. These are qualities our own church architecture would do well to recover.

# SORGHAGHTANI BEKI

(1190-1252)

*Christian Queen of the Khans*

ALONG WITH THE CHURCH OF ETHI-
opia, scholars and lay people alike have tended to ignore
Christianity in Asia, which had a vibrant life up until about
the fourteenth century. These churches, collectively referred
to as Nestorian Christianity, were considered heretical by the
churches inside the empire because they distinguished more
sharply between Christ's human and divine natures than the
Roman or Eastern Orthodox churches did. They acknowl-
edged Jesus' divinity and his true humanity, but they were
uncomfortable referring to Mary as the "mother of God"
as the liturgy had it. They argued she should be referred to

as the "mother of Christ" since she was the mother of Jesus' human nature, not his divine nature.

Nestorian Christianity spread from its center in Persia across Asia. It had a presence in China as early as the 600s AD, and in Central Asia several tribes converted to Nestorianism. Among these were the Keraits, a powerful Mongol tribe.

The Keraits took in a young man named Temujin, who would later be known as Genghis Khan, when his father was poisoned by rivals. As Temujin grew in power, the Kerait khan became worried and plotted to assassinate him. Temujin got word of this, however, and defeated the Keraits in battle (1203). The Kerait khan's brother had supported Temujin, however, and so after the battle Temujin had his son Tolui marry Sorghaghtani, a Nestorian Christian.

Because of her place in Temujin's family, Sorghaghtani became one of the most influential women in history and became known as the Mother of Great Khans.

Sorghaghtani bore Tolui four sons. When Genghis Khan died in 1227, he skipped over his first two sons and passed the title of Great Khan to his third son, Ögedai. Tolui was given authority over eastern Mongolia, northern China, and parts of Iran.

When Tolui died in 1232, Ögedai allowed her to administer her husband's lands. Because Mongol men were often away for extended periods of time, Mongol women had a great deal of authority in the household, though giving Sorghaghtani authority over her husband's estate was far from guaranteed. Ögedai, though, recognized Sorghaghtani's ability and even consulted with her on matters of state. He even proposed marriage to her; when she refused, Ögedai suggested she marry his son. She turned him down as well, claiming that she needed to devote her attention to her sons.

Things didn't always go smoothly between Sorghaghtani and her brother-in-law. She had to shame him into giving her land in Hebei province, China, which her husband had conquered and which thus should have been hers by right. Ögedai also took some of her husband's land from her along with most of her soldiers.

Ögedai died in 1241. His wife acted as regent until she engineered the election of her son as Great Khan by a *kurultai* (i.e., assembly of chiefs and khans) in 1246. The new Great Khan immediately began working to undermine the authority of his mother, Sorghaghtani, and other women leaders in the empire.

Sorghaghtani was not about to let him get away with this. She set up an alliance with the Golden Horde, the Mongol khanate that ruled the territory north of the Caspian Sea to the Balkans. In 1248, while the Great Khan was leading an army east, he died suddenly and under mysterious circumstances, possibly the victim of an assassination.

With the Great Khan's death, Sorghaghtani with the help of the Golden Horde organized a *kuraltai* which named her son Möngke Great Khan. The *kuraltai* was held in Siberia, however, not the Mongol homeland, and so its validity was challenged. Sorghaghtani then called for a new *kuraltai* in Mongolia. The Ögedai family put forward their own candidate for Great Khan, but Sorghaghtani countered that the Great Khan should be a descendant of Genghis, and the

Ögedai candidate was not. As a result, Möngke was formally named Great Khan.

Ögedai's family naturally opposed this election and tried to overthrow Möngke. He responded by arresting many members of the family and executing them. Mongol custom prohibited shedding the blood of members of a khan's family, so they were drowned or rolled in rugs and trampled by horses.

Sorghaghtani died in 1252, shortly after Möngke's elevation as Great Khan. She was buried in a Christian church with a Nestorian funeral. Even after her death, however, her legacy was far from over.

During her lifetime, Sorghaghtani was given lands to rule in her own right. She treated her non-Mongol peasant subjects well, with the result that they supported her rule and her lands prospered. This set an example that her sons would follow.

She also understood the importance of education. Although she was illiterate herself, Sorghaghtani recognized the need for literacy for administering the vast and diverse Mongol Empire, so she had her sons learn the languages of the territories they ruled. Since her son Kublai was going to inherit the family's Chinese possessions, she made sure that he understood Confucian thought as well. More broadly, Sorghaghtani was responsible for opening trade and intellectual exchange across the vast Mongol Empire.

Though she remained a Nestorian throughout her life, Sorghaghtani followed Genghis Khan in promoting religious toleration. She not only supported Christian churches, but gave alms to Muslims, Buddhists, and Confucians, following the example of the early Church in helping all in need, regardless of faith.

In addition to Möngke, two of Sorghaghtani's other sons became khans. Her second son, Kublai, inherited the family lands in China and was elected Great Khan on Möngke's death in 1259. He united China under his rule and formally declared the beginning of the Yuan Dynasty in 1271. Her third son, Hulagu, inherited the family lands in Iran, which became known as the Ilkhanate (i.e., the sub-khanate) of Persia. As Ilkhan, Hulagu expanded his territory, eventually controlling Persia, Georgia, Armenia, and Turkey. He very nearly broke Islam's control over the Middle East and might have saved the Crusader states there, but prior to the final battle Möngke died and Hulagu returned with most of his army to Mongolia to participate in the election of the new Great Khan. A greatly reduced force under his Nestorian Christian general Kitbuqa was destroyed by the Muslims at the battle of Ain Jalut, leaving the Middle East firmly in the hands of Islam.

None of Sorghaghtani's sons followed her faith, though all of them treated Christianity with great respect and, at times, even favor. Hulagu was married to a devout Christian, and as noted, his main general was also a Christian. Kublai Khan also supported the small Nestorian community in China out of respect for his mother. At one point, some Christians sided with a revolt against Kublai Khan; when the revolt was put down, Kublai Khan rebuked members of his entourage who mocked Christianity. He said that the rebels were acting unrighteously, and the Christian God therefore could not and would not support them, and so it was wrong to blame Christianity for the failure of the revolt.

Although Sorghaghtani participated in her share of bloodshed and intrigue in keeping with her era and culture, she also had a degree of wisdom and compassion for the non-Mongol poor that was very rare, and that was founded on Christian values. These qualities were also shared by Hulagu's Nestorian Christian wife: at her request, Hulagu spared the Christians in Baghdad when he sacked the city; when Möngke heard about this, he was impressed and told Hulagu that he should consult her in all his affairs.

Sorghaghtani was rightly held in high regard by people from all cultures who encountered her. Testimonies to her came from Chinese, Muslim, Persian, and both Nestorian and Roman Catholic Christian writers. For example, Bar Hebraeus, a Syrian Nestorian scholar and church leader, said of her, "If I were to see among the race of women another woman like this, I should say that the race of women was far superior to that of men."[9] Her natural talents, shaped by her faith, made her one of the most important figures in world history.

9. Moffett, *A History of Christianity in Asia*, vol. 1, 410.

# ELIZABETH OF HUNGARY

(1207-1231)

*The Queen Who Loved the Poor*

POLITICS IN THE MIDDLE AGES IN Europe was a very complicated affair. One of the central conflicts was between the pope and the Holy Roman Emperor over who was to be the supreme leader of the Christian world. In Italy, two major political parties emerged from this conflict, the Guelphs and the Ghibellines. Although initially these parties supported the pope and the emperor respectively, over time things became far more complex, with immediate political and dynastic considerations outweighing the historical positions of the parties.

In the early 1200s, the Guelph Otto IV and the Ghibelline Philip of Swabia were rivals for the imperial throne.

Landgrave Hermann I of Thuringia and King Andrew II of Hungary both supported Philip (or more precisely, opposed Otto IV), and so to strengthen their alliance the two arranged a dynastic marriage between Hermann I's oldest son, also called Hermann, and the four-year-old Elizabeth, Andrew's daughter. Elizabeth was sent to Thuringia to learn the language and customs of the region. She lived in Wartburg, the landgrave's palace where 300 years later Martin Luther would translate the New Testament into German.

Tragedy soon struck both families. Gertrude, Elizabeth's mother, was murdered in 1213 by Hungarian nobles opposed to German influence at court. Hermann I, meanwhile, kept switching sides in the wars over the imperial title, and so his land was overrun multiple times by armies from both sides. Then in 1216, Elizabeth's fiancé Hermann also died. To maintain the alliance, Elizabeth was betrothed to Ludwig IV, Hermann's younger brother. The following year, Hermann I died and Ludwig succeeded him as Landgrave of Thuringia. He was named regent of Meissen and Ostmark (Austria) in 1221, and that same year he married Elizabeth. Ludwig was twenty-one and Elizabeth fourteen.

Hermann I's court had been a center for music and poetry, pomp and politics, but Elizabeth, a religious child, preferred prayer, almsgiving, and contemplation to court life. She had taken quite a bit of abuse for this, but Ludwig protected her and put a stop to the harassment. He fully approved of Elizabeth's charitable efforts, believing that they would result in rewards in heaven. Ludwig and Elizabeth deeply loved each other and had a strong marriage. They had three children, Hermann II (1222-41), Sophia (1224-84), and Gertrude (1227-97).

Along with the wedding, the year 1221 also saw the arrival of the first Franciscan friars in Germany. Two years later, Brother Rodegar, one of the first Germans received into the order, became Elizabeth's spiritual director. From him, Elizabeth learned Francis's ideals. She was very taken with them and put them into practice with the sole exception of voluntary poverty, which her station in life prevented her from adopting. In 1225 Elizabeth founded a Franciscan friary in Eisenach, just outside of the Warburg.

Ludwig IV was a close supporter of Frederick II Hohenstaufen, who had become Holy Roman Emperor. Because of his association with Frederick, Ludwig was often away on imperial business. In the spring of 1226, he was in Cremona in northern Italy as Frederick's representative to the Imperial Diet (a convocation of representatives from the various states within the empire). While he was there, a series of disasters struck Thuringia. Floods ravaged the territory, followed by famine and a deadly epidemic.

Elizabeth, who was acting as regent in Thuringia during her husband's absence, took charge of the situation. She began distributing alms throughout the territory, even giving away state robes and jewels to help provide for the needs of her people. She built a 28-bed hospital below the Wartburg and daily went there to minister to the sick. She also distributed food daily to 900 people outside the gates of the castle. She was nineteen years old at the time.

Some members of the family seem to have been upset with Elizabeth's generosity, but when Ludwig returned, he approved all that she had done.

Stories are told of two miracles associated with Elizabeth's care for the poor. At one point when Elizabeth was carrying out bread to the poor under her cloak, some of Ludwig's relatives accused her of stealing the family's wealth to give it away—a not unreasonable suspicion given Francis of Assisi's biography[10] and Elizabeth's own actions in giving away state robes. Ludwig asked her to open her cloak to show him what she was carrying. When she did, a vision of red and white roses appeared under her cloak, the first time that roses were associated with a saint. Ludwig took this as proof that she was doing God's work.

Another story says that Elizabeth put a leper named Helias from the city of Eisenach in her own marriage bed. Her mother-in-law was horrified and told Ludwig. He was angry about this as well and went up to kick the leper out of his bed. When he pulled down the covers, however, instead of a leper he saw Christ crucified lying in the bed.

---

10. Francis believed that God called him to a life of poverty and so he began giving away the goods in his merchant father's storehouse. When his father found out, he had him hauled before the bishop in the hopes that he would talk some sense into his son. The bishop pointed out that the goods did not belong to him but to his father and the family; Francis recognized the truth in this, but in keeping with his perceived call to poverty he returned everything he had received from his father—including the clothes he wore—and walked out. The bishop hastily ordered someone to throw a cloak over him, and so he began his career as an itinerant preacher and reformer.

These stories are not intended to reflect poorly on Ludwig. He was himself a godly and generous man and supported Elizabeth's charitable work. In Thuringia, he was considered a saint himself, though he was never canonized by the Catholic church.

In 1227, the pope pressured Frederick to go on Crusade. Naturally his close friend Ludwig accompanied him. Ludwig only made it as far as Otranto in southern Italy, however, where he died of pestilence on September 11. A few weeks later, before Elizabeth had received news of her husband's death, she gave birth to Gertrude, the couple's third child.

When the news finally reached her, Elizabeth was inconsolable. She cried out, "He is dead! He is dead! The world with all its joys is dead to me!"

By this point, Elizabeth had a new spiritual director and confessor. Pope Gregory IX, who had corresponded with Elizabeth, recommended her to Conrad of Marburg, a member of the secular clergy (i.e., not a monk or friar). He was a severe man—an ascetic, a preacher of Crusade, and an inquisitor. When he became Elizabeth's confessor, he was hard on her, by our standards, even abusive. After Ludwig's death, he held her to impossibly high standards and ordered her beaten on at least some occasions when she did not measure up. That said, he was an important ally to her in the conflicts that arose after her husband's death.

Ludwig's heir was his five-year-old son Hermann II. Since he was a minor, Ludwig's brother Heinrich Raspe was appointed as his guardian and regent over Thuringia. Almost immediately trouble arose over Elizabeth's dowry. Dowries were intended to provide for a living for the wife in the event of her husband's death. Heinrich refused to return it to her, however, and Pope Gregory IX appointed Conrad of Marburg to argue Elizabeth's side in the legal conflict that followed.

In the winter after her husband's death, Elizabeth left Wartburg. Some sources say that Heinrich expelled her, but it seems more likely that she left on her own because while there she could not follow the dietary strictures laid on her by Conrad. Her aunt Matilda, who was the abbess of the Benedictine convent in the town of Kitzingen, near Würzburg, intervened and sent Elizabeth to her uncle Eckbert, who was bishop of Bamberg. Eckbert wanted her to remarry, but she refused, going so far as to threaten to cut off her nose to make herself so ugly no man would want to marry her.

Meanwhile, Ludwig's remains were brought to Bamberg. Elizabeth, still in deep mourning, had the body interred in the family vault at the monastery of Reinhardsbrunn in Thuringia.

Conrad succeeded in getting Elizabeth her dowry in cash rather than in land. She received 2,000 marks and immediately distributed a quarter of it to the poor. She wanted to follow the example of Francis and give it all away, but Conrad wisely refused to allow this.

On Good Friday in 1228, about six months after her husband's death, Elizabeth took the vows of a Third Order Franciscan sister at the Franciscan convent in Eisenach. She then traveled to Marburg, where Conrad gave her and her maids the habits that marked their formal acceptance into the order. They were among the first Franciscan tertiaries in Germany.

Because of Conrad, Elizabeth still had the rest of her dowry, so in the summer of 1228 she had the resources to build a Franciscan hospital in Marburg. Conrad continued to impose harsh disciplines on her, including sending away the attendants who had served her so faithfully. Elizabeth devoted the rest of her life to caring for the sick, working herself so hard and following such a strict ascetic lifestyle that she passed away in 1231. She was all of twenty-four years old.

Miracles were soon reported at her grave, and Conrad began championing her canonization. Four years later, on Pentecost in 1235, Gregory IX formally declared her a saint. Her tomb in Marburg became a shrine and a major pilgrimage site in Germany.

Ironically, 300 years later, her descendant Philip of Hesse became an early convert to Lutheranism. In keeping with Protestant opposition to relics and pilgrimage, he had her bones and other relics taken and scattered, though some were eventually returned to Marburg. Others rest in the Convent of St. Elizabeth in Vienna.

Whatever we may think of the stories of miracles, Elizabeth was a remarkable woman who led an amazing life in the midst of tragedy and opposition. In an age such as ours in which adulthood is being delayed longer and longer, Elizabeth is an example of what even teenagers are capable of when they take their faith and their responsibilities seriously. She is also an example of the good that wealth can do in the hands of people dedicated to serving God and others.

# ROGER BACON (C. 1214-1294)
## *Observer of the World*

IN THE PREVIOUS CHAPTER ON ROB-
ert Grosseteste, we saw how a shift in worldview toward Platonic humanism began to change the way scholars studied
the natural world.

Although Platonic humanism was developed in the cathedral schools of the twelfth century, the trends that it set in
motion were further accelerated by the "New Aristotle" that
made its way into the Latin-speaking world in the twelfth
and thirteenth centuries. Prior to this, very few works of
Aristotle were available to scholars in the West. The Muslim
world had many more Aristotelian texts thanks to the translations of Hunayn ibn Ishaq and his son discussed earlier.
Eventually, Western scholars traveling to Spain realized that
much more of the Aristotelian corpus than they had available

had survived, and the process of translating these "new" works of Aristotle into Latin began.

Aristotle was an amazingly comprehensive thinker. He produced works of philosophy, logic, science, literary criticism, politics, etc. All of these were of very high quality, and together they formed a coherent worldview that answered many of the key philosophical questions that occupied medieval philosophers and theologians.

But this raised a problem: given that Platonic humanism was the intellectual framework all these scholars used, how did one go about incorporating the New Aristotle into it? In some places it fit naturally, but in others it did not.

For example, medieval philosophy was grounded in metaphysics, the study of the nature of reality. A central question in metaphysics is the relationship of universals and particulars. Thus, we see many dogs out there (particulars), but what makes them all dogs (the universal)? Is there a single canine nature that unites all of them and makes them dogs, or do we look at all the dogs and identify common characteristics that we then use as a mental or linguistic convenience? If we take the first answer—that the universals are real and that the animals are dogs because they are expressions of the universal—we are idealists: we believe that the ground of reality is found in *ideas* or non-physical universals. If we take the second, that the individual dogs are what is real and the universal is derived from the particular, we are realists.[11] Plato, most

11. The terminology of idealist and realist applies in this way to this specific context. In other contexts, realist refers to the idea that universals are real, thus almost inverting its meaning here.

ancient philosophers, and virtually all Christian thinkers to this point were all idealists;[12] Aristotle was a realist. It was thus a challenge to figure out how to incorporate Aristotle's ideas in the Platonic humanist worldview.

The solution to this dilemma came from the Cathedral School of Laon in the form of a method of study known as the *Quaestio* (question) method.

The *Quaestio* method had four steps:

1. Ask a question.
2. List authorities who had addressed the question organized into two categories, those who answered the question *yes*, and those who answered it *no*.
3. Since it was assumed that genuine authorities would not contradict each other, the next step was to use logical and linguistic analysis of the two lists to reconcile the statements with each other as much as possible.
4. Present the solution to the question that best resolves the different opinions of the authorities.

As time went on, two additional steps were added that could be repeated as necessary:

5. Raise objections to the proposed solution.
6. Resolve the objections.

In its full, six-step form, this method became known as *scholasticism*, which properly speaking is a method of study and analysis that can (and was) applied to every subject in the medieval curriculum.

---

12. To Christian Platonists, the universals were ideas in the mind of God.

This approach was tailor-made to allow lots of new material to be incorporated into an existing body of knowledge; it had the disadvantage, however, that it assumed that ancient authors (the same word in Latin can be translated as "authorities") knew the truth about which they wrote, and thus they could be relied upon and reconciled with each other.

This idea seems strange to us today, but it made sense in its day. Not only were they well aware of their history and the loss of knowledge and skills from the ancient world, but their epistemology (i.e., philosophy of knowledge) was built upon some commonsense ideas: truth is a single thing; it is objective and knowable; it is necessary for society since any society not based on truth is based on a lie and will thus collapse; and therefore as a corollary the best guide to truth is the past, particularly successful societies in the past, since to have survived they needed to have a solid understanding of truth. Thus, ancient authors must have known what they were talking about, and since truth cannot contradict itself, neither can ancient authors.

To this, later Renaissance thinkers added the idea of the decay of nature: everything in the natural world breaks down over time. Living things are born, grow to maturity, decline, and die; even rocks erode. Human society and human knowledge are parts of the natural world and so they decay over time as well. To find truth, you have to go back to the earliest sources of any field of study, before decay has set in. This is the opposite of the modern idea that truth is found in the present or the future, but it was the view of the Middle Ages and Renaissance.

Ironically enough, the scholastic method adopted to incorporate Aristotle into the existing pool of knowledge contradicted Aristotle's own methodology. Instead of looking for truth in ancient authorities, Aristotle advocated direct observation as the foundation for knowledge. As we have seen, Robert Grosseteste understood this and began applying this approach to some extent in his own work.

Scholastic methodology also violated one of the fundamental precepts of Platonic humanism, that studying the world as it is rather than as we think it should be (or as other people think it is) can lead us to knowledge of God. Roger Bacon understood this far better than most people in his era.

Bacon came from a well-off family. He studied in Oxford, probably under Robert Grosseteste, and became a master at the university, lecturing on Aristotle. He moved from there to the University of Paris, the intellectual center of medieval Europe, for several years before returning to England and joining the Franciscan order.

As a Franciscan, Bacon no longer taught at the university, and the order had a prohibition on publishing books. In 1265, however, Cardinal Guy le Gros de Foulques, a friend of Bacon, became Pope Clement IV. The new pope requested a book from Bacon on the relationship of philosophy and theology, and Bacon responded with several books covering a range of subjects.

About a decade after the pope's death, Bacon apparently was placed under house arrest for a time but was soon released and resumed his studies at the Franciscan house in Oxford. Although the arrest has been reported as persecution of a proto-scientist by the church, there is no evidence for this. The first report of his arrest dates from eighty years after his death, so it is not certain that it even happened. If it did, it was far more likely related to other parts of his thought: He had sympathies with radical Franciscans, who believed that the church should own nothing and have no political power or authority in this world, and even his scientific work was shot through with apocalyptic speculation concerning the coming of the Antichrist, much of it tied up with astrological ideas, and the nature of the age to come.[13] His personality may also have provoked a reaction against him.

In terms of methodology, like other medieval thinkers, Bacon was open to the possibility of miracles but rejected them as an explanation for normal events. To him, reliance on supernatural explanations was a mark of intellectual

13.  Laura Smoller (University of Arkansas at Little Rock) explains: "In his circa 1266 *Opus maius*, addressed to Pope Clement IV, Bacon championed Abu Ma'shar's theories about planetary conjunctions and religious change. According to Bacon, the world would see only six major religions in its history, each symbolized by the conjunction of the planet Jupiter with one of the six other planets (including the sun and moon as planets). Only the religion indicated by Jupiter's conjunction with the moon was yet to come. That final sect had to be the lying, magical sect of Antichrist. When that sect might arrive, Bacon did not hazard a guess, but he was confident that further study of the stars would yield the answer, urging Pope Clement IV in the *Opus maius*, 'I know that if the Church should be willing to consider the sacred text and prophecies ... and should order a study of the paths of astronomy, it would gain some idea of greater certainty regarding the time of Antichrist.'" "Apocalyptic Calculators of the Later Middle Ages," Third Annual Conference of the Center for Millennial Studies, Boston, MA, December 6–8, 1998, Conference Proceedings, http://www.mille.org /publications/Confpro98/SMOLLER.PDF.

laziness. Instead, Bacon believed that natural events have natural causes, and though God may intervene to interrupt the natural flow of events, that was a special, rare event.

Bacon followed Grosseteste in arguing for first-person observation as the foundation for knowledge. Although he accepted ancient authorities, he also believed that their work should be confirmed through experience and experimentation. He also followed Grosseteste in seeing mathematics as foundational for natural philosophy (i.e., studies of the natural world) and using mathematics to quantify observations.

Bacon applied these methods to a number of fields, including astronomy and optics, where he made some of his most important observations. He studied mirrors, different kinds of lenses, and began developing a theory of refraction. He identified the visible spectrum in light refracted through drops of water and made observations that would lead to an explanation of rainbows. In conjunction with optics, he also studied the anatomy of the eye and brain.

Bacon's work in the sciences extended far beyond optics, however. He was involved in an astonishing range of activities, and predicted technological breakthroughs that are reminiscent of Leonardo da Vinci and Jules Verne. He's almost too good to be true, which has made him a character in a number of science fiction and fantasy novels as a time traveler or a wizard. For example,

- He was the first European to discuss gunpowder, which came to him in the form of firecrackers brought from China by his fellow Franciscans. He even knew the chemical makeup, though he may not have been correct about the proportions.

- He anticipated microscopes, telescopes, and eyeglasses, the last of which were invented shortly after his death.
- He also anticipated the development of hydraulics, automobiles, steamships, submarines, and flying machines.

But Bacon wasn't only involved in natural philosophy. He recognized that his methodology focused on direct observation could apply to other areas of study. In particular, he was very upset with the theologians at the University of Paris who relied primarily on Peter Lombard's *Sentences* to teach theology, and only turned to Scripture after their students' ideas had been formed by their study of the *Sentences*. To make matters worse, they refused to learn the biblical languages and instead relied on what Bacon saw as obviously defective copies of the Latin translation of the Bible.

Instead of this, Bacon advocated a text-based approach to theology that relied on studying the Bible first, and only then moving to the *Sentences*. Further, he believed that the Bible should be studied in the original languages, not just in Latin, since that was the proper way to make first-hand observations of the text. This order—Bible, then *Sentences*—became the standard at Oxford even though his emphasis on the original languages wouldn't get off the ground for nearly 300 years.

To aid in the study of Scripture, Bacon developed a very sophisticated theory of language and logic that brought together elements of philosophy (drawn from Aristotle) and theology (drawn from Augustine).

Bacon wasn't a modern scientist; like other medieval theologians, Bacon saw studying the world was a theological activity since it reveals the mind of the Creator and teaches us about his attributes (Rom. 1:20). He still relied on and respected ancient authorities, though he had a methodology in place to correct them. And the same method could be used for the study of Scripture.

In short, Bacon is another example of a man with an integrated worldview, one in which all the various elements fit together synergistically to provide a cohesive vision of the world and our place in it based on biblical ideas about the nature of humanity and of the universe. Bacon understood and applied the ideas within that worldview far more systematically than most of his contemporaries, but he was only different in the consistency of his approach, not the basic concepts behind it. This integrated vision gave the medieval mind a real advantage in understanding the meaning of this world over our way of viewing fact atomistically, cut off from moral and spiritual significance and the mind of the Maker.

# GEERT GROOTE (1340-1384)
## *Founder of the Devotio Moderna*

THE 1300s WERE A DEVASTATING
period in European history. Climate shifts were causing
major disruptions to the weather, leading to large-scale famine. Epidemic diseases were breaking out across Europe.
The papacy had moved from Rome to Avignon, and a war
had broken out between France and England that would
last more than a century. Then in 1348, plague reached the
shores of mainland Europe, wiping out over half of the continent's population within three years according to the best
estimates today.

The church was facing problems with corruption as well
during this period. Much of the upper clergy was more
concerned with wealth and power than their spiritual

responsibilities, and important church offices were effectively offered for sale (a practice known as *simony*). Many members of the clergy ignored their vows of celibacy and had concubines. Theology had become increasingly divorced from practical piety and was more concerned with abstract speculation than godly living. Most of the laity knew little about Christian doctrine beyond the absolute basics and mixed superstition liberally with their faith.

Geert Groote (pronounced *GROW-tuh*) was born in 1340 in the midst of this chaos. He was from Deventer, a city in the Netherlands that had been founded by Lebuinus, an English missionary, in 768 AD. It had grown into an important and wealthy trading city, and Groote's family was one of a handful of wealthy patricians that controlled the town government. His parents died of plague, leaving him an orphan. The family's wealth remained, however, so he had a comfortable life under the care of guardians.

He was remarkably gifted intellectually and soon left home to pursue his education at Aachen and the University of Paris, where he studied the liberal arts, philosophy and theology, canon law, medicine, astronomy, and possibly some Hebrew. He completed his degree at age eighteen and returned home, eventually teaching in Deventer. He was so well respected that he was sent on a secret mission to the pope in Avignon in 1366, and shortly thereafter took a position teaching philosophy and theology at the University of Cologne, where he enjoyed a sumptuous lifestyle.

All of this changed in 1374, when Groote contracted a life-threatening illness that forced him into some serious soul-searching. Under the influence of Henry of Calcar, a friend from the University of Paris and prior of the Carthusian monastery at Munnikhuizen, Groote resigned his positions and spent three years with Henry at his monastery.

Groote left the monastery a changed man. He converted his house in Deventer into a hospice to care for poor women and organized them into a lay religious community known as the Sisters of the Common Life. Later, he also founded a male counterpart to the Sisters, the better-known Brethren of the Common Life.

The Sisters and Brethren of the Common Life based their life around the Rule of St. Augustine, though they were lay people who took no permanent vows and who could leave the group at any time. Their spiritual life centered on the *Devotio Moderna* (best translated as "renewed devotion"), a group of practices developed by Groote. The *Devotio Moderna* emphasized four main themes: a focus on the Bible; internalizing morality by replacing the vices in your life with virtues; the "imitation of Christ," by which they meant using structured meditation to put yourself into Bible stores to allow you to identify emotionally with Christ and his Passion; and a return to the model of the early Church from the corruption of the fourteenth century. The *Devotio Moderna* was thus intensely practical, with no time for abstract, speculative theology.

The Brethren and Sisters recognized that no one could actually practice the *Devotio Moderna* alone; it required living in community with a great deal of mutual support and accountability. The Brethren and Sisters therefore lived in single-sex communities, often in a single large house, to allow times of private and corporate prayer and meditation, confession, mutual correction and support, attending Mass together, and the like.

The communities supported themselves by working. Following the customs of the area, the women mostly made and sold lace. The men, however, had other options. Given the emphasis on the Bible and early Christian writers, literacy was important to the *Devotio Moderna*. Since they could read and write, many members of the Brethren earned a living by copying manuscripts and by starting schools with the goal of promoting Church renewal by enabling more people to read the sources of the Christian life themselves.

The best-known book produced by the Brethren of the Common Life was *The Imitation of Christ*, written c. 1418-1427 by Thomas à Kempis. The book was circulated widely in manuscript before its first printed edition in 1471; by 1500 it had been printed in over a hundred editions, including translations into German, French, Italian, and Spanish. The book's instructions on spiritual formation, drawn from the *Devotio Moderna*, have been enormously influential for both Catholic and Protestant spirituality. It is easily the most important devotional book in Church history next to the Bible itself.

Along with starting the Sisters and the Brethren of the Common Life, Groote was ordained as a deacon and in 1379 was appointed to be an itinerant preacher by the reform-minded bishop of Utrecht. His sermons proved very popular with the laity. Groote was more concerned about the sins of the clergy, however, since they set the spiritual tone for the entire community. With the bishop's support, he began preaching strenuously against the full range of clerical abuses. The clergy struck back: they accused him of heterodox teaching and pressured the bishop to ban all preaching by anyone other than a fully ordained priest. Groote appealed the ban and the accusation to the pope. Unfortunately, Groote died ministering to plague victims before his appeal could be heard.

Groote's significance is less in his preaching than in the vision of Church reform that inspired it, and in the institutions he created to promote that vision. In particular, the Brethren were crucial to the spread of literacy in northern Europe. Not only did they build libraries in their communities and copy manuscripts, but they also were among the first to adopt the printing press, installing one at Deventer in about 1477.

The schools set up by the Brethren of the Common Life were even more important than their production of books. The Brethren spread throughout the Hanseatic League—an alliance of trading cities in the Netherlands and northern Germany—and from there moved into central Germany as well. And wherever the Brethren went, they established schools. In the fifteenth and early sixteenth centuries, nearly everyone in this part of Europe who received a primary school education went to a school operated by the Brethren of the Common Life. This includes the great Christian humanist Desiderius Erasmus, who attended the Deventer school, and Martin Luther, who went to the school in Magdeburg.

Groote saw education as an essential part of his greater goal of Church renewal. Although it took over a century, the education provided in the schools he inspired laid the groundwork for both reform in the Catholic church and the rise and spread of Protestantism. But the schools of the Brethren were more than nurseries for Church reform. They turned northern Germany into a literate culture for the first time in history, which developed a market for books that helped inspire Gutenberg in the creation of movable metal type and the printing press.

Groote's educational program thus had enormous implications beyond Church reform and character-building. It provided northern Europe with the tools to advance in all areas of learning, including mathematics, astronomy, law, politics, and the arts, and laid the groundwork for the spread of Renaissance ideas into the empire. Historic Christianity teaches that all truth is God's truth, all areas of life are sacred, and thus all can and should be studied as a means of honoring God. Even if it was not the initial intent, these results of Groote's education program were in keeping with his goal of reforming Church and society through a more thoroughgoing understanding of the Bible and the biblical worldview.

# ABBA ENBAQOM/ABUL-FATH

## (C. 1470-C. 1561)

### *Champion of Ethiopia*

ANCIENT CHRISTIAN COMMUNITIES
in the Middle East today are under assault as never before
by Islamic forces. At the same time, unprecedented numbers of Muslims are coming to faith in Jesus Christ as a
result of dreams in which Issa (Jesus) appears to them.
Although the pace at which these two trends are happen-
ing is accelerating, neither is a new phenomenon. Nor are
Christian apologetics to Islam new; medieval Christians in
the Middle East and Europe developed arguments for the
truth of Christianity over Islam. All of these elements are
part of the life story of Abba Enbaqom, whose birth name
was Abul-Fath.

Abul-Fath was born in Yemen to a Jewish mother and a noble father and was raised as a Muslim. Even as a young man he began to express doubts about his religion and began to investigate Islam and its literature. His doubts eventually alienated him from his parents. In 1489, he went to Ethiopia as a merchant, accompanying a freed Ethiopian captive. He stayed in northern Ethiopia for three years and then moved south to the capital for two more years.

During this period, Abul-Fath continued his religious investigations. In 1494 he received a revelation in which he was told, "You are not following the right path; go to the Abima Marcos, who is head of the priests of Ethiopia, and he will teach you another path."[14]

Abima Marcos thus seems to have been involved in Abul-Fath's conversion, though the most important person was Echage Petros. Echage is the title of the abbot of Debre Libanos, the most important monastery in Ethiopia, and is the second highest office in the Ethiopian church. Echage Petros taught Abul-Fath the faith and baptized him under the name "Enbaqom" (Habakkuk).

Enbaqom decided to stay in the monastery and began academic studies. He mastered Coptic, Armenian, Syriac, and Hebrew, and later added Portuguese, the Venetian dialect of Italian, and Latin. He had already learned Arabic and Ge'ez, the language of Ethiopia. Among other things,

---

14. Francisco Álvares, *Verdadera Informaçam das terras do Preste Joam das Indias* (Lisbon: Luís Rodrigues, 1540), translated as *The Prester John of the Indies*, ed. C.F. Beckingham and G.W.B. Huntingford (Cambridge University Press for the Hakluyt Society, 1961), 262–263.

he translated John Chrysostom's commentary on Hebrews from Arabic into Ge'ez, as well as the Apocalypse of John, the Indian story *Barlaam and Josaphat*, and several other works. As a result, he greatly enriched the theology of the Ethiopian church. His learning and character were so highly regarded that upon the death of Petros he was selected as the new Echage, the only non-Ethiopian to ever hold that position (c. 1523).

Unfortunately, however, possibly because of his ethnic origin, he had many enemies in the monastery. In 1526 he was accused by a group of his monks of disloyalty to Emperor Lebna Dengel. Enbaqom was sentenced to death, although the emperor's sisters prevailed upon him to commute the sentence to exile.

Three years later, the Adal Sultanate in Somalia launched a war against Ethiopia with the intention of conquering the country and forcing its conversion to Islam. The invasion was led by Ahmad ibn Ibrahim al-Ghazi, nicknamed Gragn (the left-handed), a Somali imam and general possibly of Arab extraction. Ahmad Gragn was supplied by the Ottoman Turks with muskets and cannons, weapons that had not been seen in Ethiopia prior to this. Partly due to the psychological impact of gunpowder weapons and partly due to their firepower, Ahmad Gragn consistently defeated the Ethiopian forces sent against him, leaving Lebna Dengel unable to face the invaders in pitched battle.

At about the time of the invasion, Lebna Dengel pardoned Enbaqom and offered him his old position as Echage. Enbaqom refused and continued his exile, moving from place to place to avoid Ahmad Gragn's troops and providing comfort and leadership to the Christian community.

Ahmad Gragn's armies were rampaging across the Ethiopian highlands, converting people at the point of the sword and destroying churches and monasteries. Among other things, they captured and sacked Lalibela, including the monolithic churches there, destroyed the Church of Our Lady of Mount Zion in Axum, built by King Ezana and the traditional site of imperial coronations, and burned the great monastery at Debra Libanos. In the twelve years that he occupied the highlands, Ahmad Gragn's army destroyed the work of centuries in the churches, monasteries, and libraries they burned.

Enbaqom was so upset by the destruction that he wrote a letter in Arabic to Ahmad Gragn in 1532. Citing the Quran, Enbaqom urged Ahmad Gragn not to destroy churches and monasteries and not to kill priests and monks. Ahmad Gragn evidently replied that he was obligated to respect the Torah and the Gospels, and so he would not destroy churches and would only kill those who resisted him. On the other hand, he also began hunting for Enbaqom with the intention of capturing and executing him.

Enbaqom, possibly believing that Ethiopia would fall to Ahmad Gragn, expanded his letter into the book *Anqaṣa Amin* (*Gateway of Faith*). This book, which draws on his extensive knowledge of the Quran and Islamic literature, makes a clear argument for the superiority of Christianity over Islam. He rehearses the standard objections of Arab Christians to Islam but adds several of his own; he also gives an account of his conversion. It was an audacious move: he seems to have been trying to convert Ahmad Gragn to Christianity.

Enbaqom's background in Islam and his familiarity with Judaism through his mother enabled him to teach the Ethiopian Christians how to think about and respond to Islam, with the result that the Ethiopian church increasingly saw his presence as providential in helping keep the kingdom from converting to Islam.

Meanwhile, Lebna Dengel realized that he had no chance to stop Ahmad Gragn without European help. The Portuguese had arrived in the Indian Ocean, and with their superior ships had diverted the spice trade away from its traditional routes through the Middle East to Lisbon. In fact, as early as the 1520s Enbaqom had made the acquaintance of the Portuguese priest Francisco Àlvares. And so Lebna Dengel appealed to the Portuguese for help. Before help could arrive, however, he died in battle against Ahmad Gragn (1540).

Lebna Dengel's successor Galawdewos (Claudius) recalled Enbaqom and apologized for his father's mistreatment of the abbot. He made Enbaqom a councilor in war. Enbaqom seems to have influenced Galawdewos's *Confession of Faith*, which represented a diplomatic response to the Catholic church that helped ensure continued Portuguese support but maintained the independence of the Ethiopian church.

Meanwhile, the Portuguese arrived in 1541 with a 400-strong contingent of musketeers. To make a long story short, they made better use of their muskets than the Somalis did, and this contingent began to turn the tide of the war. Both sides had to call for more reinforcements, in the case of the Somalis from the Turks, but in the end Ahmad Gragn was wounded and later killed in battle (1543), bringing an end to the threat to Ethiopia from Somalia. Galawdewos's successor Menas (r. 1559-1563) had Enbaqom restored to the office of Echage, which he held until his death in c. 1561.

In our age where we are again seeing slaughter of Christians, desecration of churches, and the destruction of major cultural artifacts such as the Buddhas of Bamiyan by the Taliban or the ancient Assyrian statues in Iraq currently being destroyed by the Islamic State, it is important to remember that these actions are not new or isolated events historically. But we also need to remember that the current movement of conversions in the Islamic world by dreams and visions is also not a new event: God has been working for centuries among Muslims, though in ways that are not generally visible. Enbaqom is an example of this, as well as an example of faithfulness in the midst of a war of extermination against the Church and of active engagement with the persecutors using words and the weapons of the Spirit. May he be an encouragement and model for the suffering Christians in the Middle East and elsewhere in the Muslim world today.

# REFORMATION ERA

EUROPE CHANGED IN A RANGE OF ways after the chaos of the fourteenth century discussed in the previous chapter on Geert Groote. The Italian Renaissance that emerged in the wake of the Black Death had profound effects on art and scholarship. The printing press was invented in Germany, creating a revolution in communication, education, and learning unrivaled until the invention of the internet. Portuguese explorers found their way around Africa and took control of the lucrative spice trade with Asia, beginning the Atlantic slave trade as well. Columbus linked the old world of Europe, Africa, and Asia with the new world of the Americas, a world-changing event in a way that previous voyages between the continents had not been.

All was not well in the church, however. After the Great Schism of the West, which featured two and then three competing popes, each backed by different kingdoms, the papacy was largely seen as just another Italian principality, but one that also happened to be the head of the "universal" Church. The Renaissance papacy was a byword for corruption, with popes engaging in widespread nepotism up to and including making the pope's illegitimate son a cardinal and seeking to turn papal lands into an independent state under that illegitimate son. The cardinals who served in the papal court were ambitious, power-hungry, and greedy for the most part, though occasionally a reformer would be elevated to a cardinalship. Bishops were typically younger sons of important nobles who looked at their position as an honorable way to make a good living and a way to enhance family power. Local priests were not allowed to marry but frequently had concubines, a fact that their parishioners found comforting because it meant they were less likely to molest or seduce their wives or daughters. Monks were proverbially drunks.

Despite the problems, the Catholic church's position in Europe was unassailable because it had a monopoly on one product everyone wanted: salvation. As long as western Europeans believed that their only hope of salvation was the Catholic church, no matter how corrupt the church became, its position was secure.

It was secure, that is, until Martin Luther broke the monopoly with his rediscovery of the doctrine of justification by grace alone through faith alone.

Luther ignited a firestorm of controversy. His challenge to the Catholic church may have been theological, but because in this period religion affected every area of life, Luther's reform had political, social, and cultural implications that went far beyond what we would think of as religious matters. Among many other things, Luther's emphasis on the priesthood of all believers broke down the sacred/secular divide by declaring that all people had direct access to God without a priest as their mediator. Pastors had their role, but in principle they were no more important or holy than cobblers who provided an essential service by making shoes to keep their neighbors' feet warm.

Because Luther believed that all theological questions were to be settled by Scripture interpreted according to the "Rule of Faith" (essentially, the Creeds), he also believed it was important for everyone as well as priests to be able to read the Bible. He thus championed universal basic education, including for girls.

The Reformation also transformed family life. One major change involved the end of the requirement for clerical celibacy and thus the closing of monasteries and convents. Marriage thus became the norm for everyone. The father as the head of the household was the "first pastor" for the family and was responsible not only for their physical welfare but their spiritual welfare as well.

The Catholic church had no effective response to the rise of Protestantism for nearly twenty-five years after Luther triggered the Reformation by posted the *Ninety-Five Theses* (1517). With the founding of the Society of Jesus (i.e., the Jesuits), reforms at the papal court, and crackdowns on any challenges to its authority, the Catholic church began to recover territory lost to Protestantism and to engage in foreign missions through the Spanish and Portuguese colonies in the New World and Asia.

# MARGUERITE
# D'ANGOULÊME (1492-1549)
## *Protector of Protestants*

CHARLES, COUNT OF ANGOULÊME, was a Prince of the Blood, that is, a member of the royal family of France descended from Charles V (r. 1364-1380). He married Louise of Savoy when she was eleven years old, though they did not live together until she was fifteen. They soon had their first child, Marguerite, and two years later, in 1494, their second child, Francis, who by dynastic accident was the second in line to the French throne should Charles VIII die without a surviving heir.

Charles of Angoulême died in 1496, leaving Louise a widow at age nineteen. Louise was an unusually well-educated young woman and particularly adept at diplomacy; she saw to it that the same was true of Marguerite and Francis. In the course of her education, Marguerite was exposed to the Bible and developed a love of the Scriptures.

Marguerite was married at age seventeen to Charles IV, Duke of Alençon, on orders from Louis XII of France. This was a matter of political expediency: Louis XII wanted to keep the duchy of Alençon in the family. It was a poor match: Charles was close to illiterate and the couple had nothing in common.

Louis XII also named Marguerite's brother Francis as his heir and had him marry his daughter Claude. He came to the throne as Francis I in 1515. At that point, Marguerite became one of the most important women in France, second only to her mother Louise of Savoy. Marguerite became known for her learning, kindness, and generosity, and her home became internationally recognized as a center of scholarship and culture. Marguerite herself had by this time learned Greek, Latin, Hebrew, Italian, Spanish, and German, along with her native French.

In 1525, Francis was campaigning in Italy when he met a crushing defeat at the hands of Charles V's forces at the Battle of Pavia. Many of the leading nobles of France were killed and Francis himself was captured. Marguerite's husband Charles IV of Alençon led the remnants of the French forces north of the Alps. He was unfairly blamed for the defeat at Pavia and died soon thereafter.

While in captivity in Spain, Francis became gravely ill. Marguerite, now a widow, went to him, riding twelve hours per day in the middle of winter to make it to Francis before her safe conduct expired. Francis recovered, and Marguerite returned to Paris. Francis would be released soon thereafter after being forced into the humiliating Treaty of Madrid (1526), which he repudiated as soon as he returned to France.

In 1527, Marguerite married Henry II d'Albret, King of Navarre. Navarre was a small kingdom that had straddled the Pyrenees. In 1512, however, Ferdinand II of Aragon invaded Navarre and annexed all its territory south of the Pyrenees; Navarre was thus reduced to an area in the southwestern part of modern France. Marguerite now spent most of her time in Pau and Nérac in her husband's kingdom, though she remained very close to her brother.

France was undergoing important cultural changes during this period. Francis I had brought back from Italy a new approach to education known in the period as the "New Learning" and today as Renaissance humanism; he also paid handsomely to have Italian intellectuals such as Leonardo da Vinci relocate to France. From these scholars, Marguerite had developed a love for Dante and Renaissance literature, including particularly Petrarch and Boccaccio. Other scholars in France, particularly in legal studies, began harnessing the skills of the Italian humanists in their own fields and, with that, began advocating societal reform with the support of the king. In France, the Catholic church was so intertwined with the social and political fabric that reforming society meant reforming the church.

And therein lay the problem.

Luther had posted the *Ninety-Five Theses* just two years after Francis had ascended the throne, and Lutheran ideas were spreading in France. These mingled with humanist and indigenous reform ideas to create "a period of magnificent religious anarchy," as one historian described it.[15] Marguerite herself was an *évangelique*, not quite a Protestant but with clear Protestant sympathies, a commitment to Scripture, and a desire for church reform. Francis himself seems to have leaned in that direction up to a point as well: he was an avid supporter of humanism but detested heresy. It never seems to have occurred to him that the two could mix.

The Sorbonne—the theological faculty of the University of Paris—was committed to a conservative form of Catholicism and disliked and distrusted even Catholic humanist reformers. Supported by the *Parlement* of Paris (a law court rather than a legislative body), the Sorbonne brought suspected Protestants up on heresy charges. If convicted, they were typically burned alive in the public square.

The Sorbonne and the *Parlement* accused many prominent French humanists and reformers of heresy, but they did not count on Marguerite's influence at court. Marguerite convinced her brother on multiple occasions to prohibit the *Parlement* from taking action in heresy trials. She was not always successful, but she did save a number of prominent reformers from execution.

Along with intervening in the trials in Paris, Marguerite made her court at Nérac a refuge for humanists and Protestants fleeing persecution. Jacques Lefèvre d'Étaples, the great

15. *A New Kind of History and Other Essays: Lucien Febvre*, ed. Peter Burke, and trans. K. Folca (London: Routledge and Kegan Paul, 1973; repr. New York: Harper and Row, 1973), 85–86.

humanist reformer whose *Commentaries on the Epistles of Paul* (1512) articulated the doctrine of justification by faith several years before Luther, was taken in by Marguerite when he was accused of heresy. John Calvin also made his way to Nérac when he fled from Paris in the face of a heresy accusation as well. Marguerite would later take an interest in Calvin's career in Geneva. These are only two of the many refugees from persecution that Marguerite would take in and protect.

Along with being a refuge for religious reformers, Nérac also became a cultural center under Marguerite. Artists, writers, and scholars all benefited from her patronage there, including François Rabelais, Clément Marot, and Pierre de Ronsard. Rabelais would dedicate book 3 of *Gargantua and Pantagruel* to Marguerite.

Marguerite was also a writer herself who helped shape the French language. Along with poems and plays, she wrote two particularly important books. The first, *The Mirror of the Sinful Soul* (1531), was a devotional work that she wrote after the death of her son. In it, Marguerite presents herself as a sinner and explores all the ways in which she has betrayed God, yet in the midst of her guilt and unworthiness, she always ends with grace. Marguerite's reflections are informed by Augustinian and Pauline theology and are compatible with Protestantism. Not surprisingly, the Sorbonne condemned the work as heretical. When Marguerite heard about this, she protested to Francis, who forced the Sorbonne to rescind the condemnation and apologize to Marguerite. He also took away its right to approve the publication of theological works.

When she was twelve years old, Elizabeth Tudor, later Queen Elizabeth I of England, translated *The Mirror of the Sinful Soul* for Catherine Parr. It is possible that Elizabeth inherited her copy from her mother Anne Boleyn, who had spent years in the French court and likely knew Marguerite.

Among literary rather than religious scholars, Marguerite is best remembered for the *Heptameron*, a book based on Boccaccio's *Decameron*. It tells the story of a group of people trapped by a flood who decide to pass the time by telling each other stories. Like the *Decameron*, it was intended to have one hundred short stories in it, but Marguerite had only completed seventy-two before her death. Some of the stories are pious, others are bawdy in the extreme. This combination seems out of place today, especially given Marguerite's religious sensibilities, but in the sixteenth century it was not at all unusual.

Marguerite's spirituality was influenced by Protestant thinkers including Luther and Calvin, by humanists such as Lefèvre, by Renaissance Neoplatonists, and others, and thus her faith defies easy categorization. Although she never broke formally with Rome, she supported reformers who did. In many ways, she illustrates a middle ground among French reformers who supported neither Rome nor Geneva. She combined pietistic mysticism, a focus on the Bible, and a concern for living out the faith in practical ways. For example, in addition to protecting reformers, she worked to help the needy in Navarre with the support of her husband. She called herself "the Prime Minister of the

Poor" and was famous for her almsgiving and her efforts to help raise the poor out of poverty.

Marguerite's only surviving child, Jeanne d'Albret, became Queen of Navarre in 1555. She converted to Protestantism under the influence of Calvin's successor in Geneva, the French nobleman Theodore Beza. Jeanne's son Henry de Navarre would become King Henry IV of France.

Marguerite was born with many advantages, and circumstances added to her influence. Unlike many in similar situations, Marguerite made the best of the opportunities her position presented to her. She is recognized as the "Mother of the French Renaissance" for her support of writers and her own poetry and prose; she protected religious reformers (even those with whom she had disagreements) and did her best to moderate the harshness of her brother's religious policy; and she lived out her faith in practical ways, walking the streets of her capital unescorted, talking to anyone who came to her, giving alms to the poor and promoting their interests at court. While few of us have the opportunities she had, she is a model of how we can do our best to do good in all of the circumstances life presents us.

## SOURCES

Philip Edgcumbe Hughes, *Lefèvre: Pioneer of Ecclesiastical Renewal in France* (Grand Rapids: Eerdmans, 1984).

William Monter, *Judging the French Reformation: Heresy Trials by Sixteenth Century Parlements* (Cambridge, MA: Harvard University Press, 1999).

Susan Snyder, "Guilty Sisters: Marguerite de Navarre, Elizabeth of England, and *Le Miroir de l'ame pechereuse*," http://freessays.0catch.com/lizsnyder.html.

Paula Summers, "Marguerite d'Angoulême," *Encyclopedia of the Reformation* (New York and Oxford: Oxford University Press, 1996).

Thierry Wanegffelen, *Ni Rome ni Genève: les fidèles entre deux chaires en France au XVIe siècle* (Geneva: Slatkine, 1997).

# KATHERINA SCHÜTZ ZELL

(1497/8-1562)

*Pastor's Wife and Theologian*

KATHERINA SCHÜTZ WAS BORN IN Strasbourg, then part of the Holy Roman Empire, in 1497 or 1498. She was the youngest of five children, two boys and three girls. Though not part of the city's elite, the family was reasonably well off and was able to provide all the children including Katherina with a good education. She was able to read and write German well, and she learned Latin later, probably from her husband.

Even as a girl, Katherina was very interested in religion. Then, in 1518, a young priest named Matthew Zell was appointed by the Catholic bishop of Strasbourg to the Cathedral of St. Lawrence. Zell was a follower of Luther, whose

*Ninety-Five Theses* had been published the year before and circulated widely. Zell began teaching Luther's understanding of salvation from the pulpit, and from Zell's preaching and Luther's writings, Katherina adopted Lutheran theology as her own.

Up to this point, virtually all of the clergy in Europe had been celibate, whether as Catholic priests or as newly minted Protestant pastors, and that was what people expected of their clergy. But Luther had taught that marriage was an honorable estate and that there was no biblical reason clergy had to be celibate. And so, five years after Zell arrived, he and Katherina got married, making him one of the first Protestant pastors to marry. They even beat Luther to the altar by two years.

The marriage was controversial, though, since it felt wrong even to Protestants to have married clergy. When the bishop heard about it, he excommunicated Matthew Zell. Further, rumors began to circulate of infidelity. In response, Katherina vigorously defended their marriage and pointed out the rampant sexual irregularities that were well known among the Catholic clergy.

This incident points to an important element in the Zells' marriage: it was a partnership among equals in an era in which women were expected to be silent and submissive. Matthew understood Katherina's gifts and talents and allowed her full scope to exercise them.

Katherina Zell took very seriously the responsibility of presbyters to exercise hospitality. Their home became a haven for visiting reformers and Protestant refugees. Many French

Protestants made their way to Strasbourg to escape persecution, including John Calvin, whom she hosted in her home. Katherine not only took care of their physical needs but also actively participated in their theological discussions. She was so astute in her theological understanding that many reformers considered her more knowledgeable than some university-trained theologians.

In this period Strasbourg was far more tolerant of different religious views than most other places; Martin Bucer, the principal reformer of the city, was well known for his irenic disposition. The Zells were even more tolerant than most others: Matthew commented that he would welcome into his home anyone who recognized Jesus as the Son of God and the only Savior of the world. Even Anabaptists, who were considered heretics by most Protestants and Catholics, were welcome. Katherina strongly supported her husband's attitude toward religious toleration.

Katherina went beyond taking care of the visitors in her home, however. She was very active in what Bucer would label the diaconal branch of the ministry: taking care of the poor, the sick, widows, and orphans. In one incident, a local magistrate came down with leprosy and had to be quarantined. Katherina visited him and wrote letters to encourage him. She also became an advocate for victims of persecution. She was so effective in this role that her husband named her "Church Mother of Strasbourg."

Katherina also became involved in the reform outside of Strasbourg. A Protestant minister in the nearby town of Kensingen was forced to flee due to religious persecution.

one hundred and fifty men from his church accompanied him, but when they returned, they found the gates of the city locked against them. They were pursued, and one was killed. The rest fled to Strasbourg.

Katherina saw to it that most of them found beds, many in her own home. And she wrote a tract entitled *Letter to the suffering women of the community of Kentzingen, who believe in Christ, sisters with me in Jesus Christ* to try to comfort the wives whose husbands were now in exile.

This was Katherina's first public work, but it was far from her last. Katherina was a prolific writer of pamphlets, an essential tool for communicating the message of Protestantism in her day. Many of her letters and pamphlets were devoted to comforting the wives of Protestant leaders who had to spend extended periods away from their families. She also wrote catechetical instructions, devotional writings, biblical meditations, and a sermon; she even participated in written theological debates with male theologians and corresponded with reformers in other parts of Europe.

She also was involved in the publication of the hymnal of the Bohemian Brethren, the descendants of the Hussites, proto-Protestants from Bohemia. Like Luther, she realized that music was a powerful tool for the spread of the Reformation. The texts of the hymns were unalterable due to the wishes of their author, but Katherina oversaw new musical settings for them and also wrote the introduction to the hymnal. She ended up being the most published woman theologian of the Reformation.

Of course, as a woman, taking this kind of public role brought on a great deal of criticism from traditionalists who believed that women should be silent and submissive to their husband. Her reply was twofold. First, although Paul talked about women being silent in church, Joel said that God's menservants and maidservants would prophesy; in light of this, she didn't see herself as John the Baptist rebuking the Pharisees, but as Balaam's ass rebuking his master. Second, everything she did, she did with the full support and consent of her husband; she was thus not violating any biblical precepts dealing with submission by her writings.

Unfortunately, Katherina faced a serious sorrow in her personal life: her only two children died in infancy. She interpreted this as punishment by God. When her husband died in 1548, she was heartbroken but nonetheless spoke at his funeral. Bucer sent her to Basel to stay with a young pastor and his wife, but she soon decided to return home in Strasbourg to continue her biblical studies and works of mercy.

That same year, the First Schmalkaldic War between the Catholic Emperor Charles V of Habsburg and the Protestant princes in the empire ended in a smashing imperial victory. Charles was determined to restore the Protestant heretics to the Catholic fold, but he recognized that this needed to be handled with some care. He issued a religious settlement known as the Augsburg Interim. Unfortunately, Bucer had enough differences with the Lutherans that the terms of the Interim made his position in Strasbourg untenable. Katherina kept him and several other reformers hidden in her house until Bucer was able to go into exile to England in 1549.

In the midst of all this turmoil, Katherina continued her work. She continued her writing and her biblical studies as well as her works of mercy. In 1562, in keeping with her earlier practice of toleration, she conducted the funeral of a follower of Caspar Schwenkfeld, a spiritualist and Anabaptist, since there was no one else in the city willing to do it. She was quite ill herself at the time and died shortly thereafter.

Katherina Schütz Zell was one of several formidable women who were wives of Protestant reformers. Given the dangers of that era and the larger-than-life personalities of some of the reformers, it is not surprising that they had wives with equally strong personalities. In Katherina Zell's case, her voice was even more prominent than her husband's, even though she was careful not to overstep the boundaries she saw in Scripture for her as a wife and as a woman. That she believed Scripture gave her far more latitude than most people of her day recognized made her all the more remarkable as she sought to balance her calling, her understanding and interpretation of Scripture, and her commitment based on that understanding of the Bible to remain under her husband's authority.

# ROQUE GONZÁLEZ
# DE SANTA CRUZ (1576-1628)
*Jesuit Missionary to the Guaraní*

MISSIONARIES—BOTH CATHOLIC AND Protestant—are frequently portrayed as being tools of the colonial powers, working hand-in-glove with European states to subjugate the indigenous people of their colonies and destroying their cultures. While there is no question that this was true of some missionaries, it was not true of many others. Roque González de Santa Cruz and his successors are examples of missionaries who worked to protect native peoples and who respected their cultures while at the same time bringing Christianity to them.

Roque González was born in Asunción, Paraguay, the son of a Spanish noble family. He was a religious child who seemed destined for the priesthood. He was ordained as a priest at age twenty-three, somewhat reluctantly since he did not think he was worthy of the office.

He had learned the Guarani language, and so he soon began doing mission work among the native peoples. In 1609, he joined the Society of Jesus to have more opportunities to engage in missionary activities and to avoid ecclesiastical promotion.

The Jesuits were relatively late arrivals to the mission fields of South America, so they were forced to do their work in the frontier areas of the colonies. This suited Fr. Roque's interests and linguistic ability, and may have contributed to his decision to join the order.

Many of the native tribes were suspicious of missionaries. They were afraid that if the priests came in, hordes of Europeans would follow. Fr. Roque worked very hard at building trust with the tribes, and so he and a few other Jesuits were allowed to begin to minister in the area.

At this point, the Spanish colonists were abusing and enslaving the natives (contrary to Spanish law), and the Portuguese were even worse. The Jesuits saw the oppression of the natives as a real impediment to conversion, and so with the blessing of the crown they began to create "reductions," that is, communities of native peoples who would be protected from molestation by the colonial powers. The earliest reduction was the Loreta Reduction, founded on the Rio Paranápanema in 1609; the next, the Reduction San Ingacio Guazú, was founded in 1611 by Roque González.

These reductions were autonomous native communities governed by the Jesuits and native chiefs. Unlike most reductions, which forced the native peoples to adopt European customs, the Jesuit reductions allowed their inhabitants to hold on to much of their traditional culture.

The Jesuit reductions had a solid economic foundation built on communal farming combined with private property. They eventually also developed a wide range of manufacturing and crafts, including making fine musical instruments that were exported to Europe. The reductions thus became economically successful communities operating autonomously within the Spanish colonial empire.

Most importantly, the reductions provided protection against European slavers and other marauders. As a result, entire bands of native people flocked to the reductions, which collectively reached a population of 80,000 or more.

Fr. Roque described the Reduction San Ignacio Guazú as follows:

> This town had to be built from its very foundations. In order to do away with occasions of sin, I decided to build it in the style of the Spaniards, so that everyone should have his own house, with fixed boundaries and a corresponding yard. This system prevents easy access from one house to another, which used to be the case and which gave occasion for drunken orgies and other evils.
>
> A church and parish house are being erected for our needs. Comfortable and enclosed with an adobe wall, the houses are built with cedar girders—cedar is very common wood here. We have worked hard to arrange all this. But with even greater zest and energy—in fact

with all our strength—we have worked to build temples to Our Lord, not only those made by hands but spiritual temples as well, namely the souls of these Indians.

On Sundays and feast days we preach during mass, explaining the catechism beforehand with equal concern for boys and girls. The adults are instructed in separate groups of about 150 men and the same number of women. Shortly after lunch, we teach them reading and writing for about two hours.

There are still many non-Christians in this town. Because of the demands of planting and harvesting all cannot be baptized at the same time. So every month we choose those best prepared.... Among the 120 or so adults baptized this year there were several elderly shamans.[16]

Not content with building one reduction to reach the native population, Fr. Roque went on to found six additional reductions in the region.

The Jesuit reductions were very successful—so successful that they began to attract the unwanted attention of the colonial powers. Some of the reductions were in Portuguese territories, and Portugal had no qualms about enslaving the native peoples. As a result, these reductions were often attacked by slavers. In 1630 alone, it is estimated that 30,000 natives were killed or enslaved.

16.   Bert Ghezzi, *Voices of the Saints: A 365-Day Journey with Our Spiritual Companions* (Chicago: Loyola Press, 2000), 536–37, https://www.ignatianspirituality.com/ignatianvoices/16th-and-17th-century -ignatian-voices/t-roque-gonzalez-sj/.

The following year, the Jesuits moved the reductions out of Portuguese territory to Uruguay and gained permission from the crown to develop militias to defend them against the slavers. In 1641, Portuguese slavers crossed the border to raid the reductions, but they were soundly defeated by the local militia. The militia's cavalry was particularly effective. They wore European-style uniforms and carried bows and arrows along with muskets.

The Treaty of Madrid (1750) ceded yet more Spanish territory to Portugal, placing more of the reductions into Portuguese territory. The Jesuits once again tried to move the populace, but Sepé Tiaraju, a mission-born Guarani, led a revolt against the Spanish. The Guarani were so successful that the Spanish were forced to sign an armistice with them. Two years later, however, a combined Spanish-Portuguese army crushed the Guarani militia, killing an estimated 1,500 Indians.

The colonial powers now considered the Jesuits and the reductions a threat. In 1767, the Jesuits were expelled from Spanish territories, and in the aftermath the reductions withered away or were absorbed into colonial culture.

Fr. Roque did not live to see these developments, however.

In 1628, Fr. Roque was joined by two young Spanish Jesuits, Alonso Rodriguez and Juan de Castillo. They founded a reduction named Asuncion de Iyui on the Ijuhi River. Leaving Fr. Castillo there, Fr. Roque and Fr. Rodriguez pushed on into what is now Brazil and founded a reduction at Caaro.

Unfortunately, Ñezú, one of the local shamans, opposed the Jesuits' attempt to move into his area. Apparently, the

Jesuits were so successful in converting the natives that they were eroding Ñezú's position in the region. He incited Nheçu, the chief of the tribe, to attack the Jesuits at their newly constructed church. Fr. Roque was raising a bell into the tower when one of the tribesmen snuck up behind him and killed him with a tomahawk. Fr. Rodriguez heard the noise and came in to investigate. He was struck down as well and the church burned. Nheçu then led his men upriver, where they attacked Fr. Castillo. He was tied up, beaten, and stoned to death.

They were recognized as martyrs and officially canonized by Pope John Paul II in 1988.

Fr. Roque and the Jesuits with him worked very hard to balance three sometimes conflicting aims: convert the Indians, bring in the best parts of European culture to improve their lives, and allow as much of the native culture as possible to shape the life of the community. They have been criticized for being excessively paternalistic or for creating a theocratic tyranny, but in the period even anti-Catholic and anti-Jesuit authors such as Voltaire and Rousseau praised the freedom and autonomy of the reductions. And considering the alternative was slaughter or enslavement, the reductions were an important step in trying to protect the native peoples from the worst depredations of the colonists. It is thus unfair to criticize them for not doing things the way we would have liked them to.

# MARTIN DE PORRES (1579-1639)
*Healer and Servant of the Poor*

FOLLOWING PIZARRO'S CONQUEST
of Peru (1532), the Spanish crown decided it needed more
control over its colony. In 1542, Peru was reorganized as a
viceroyalty under the viceroy Francisco de Toledo. From the
Spanish capital in Lima, Francisco de Toledo instituted a
system of forced labor to exploit the region's silver mines,
making the colony the center of Spanish wealth and power
in South America.

As was the case in other Spanish colonies, Peruvian society
in this period was very conscious of race, with the Spanish
seen as clearly superior to others and judging the rest by their
ethnicity and skin tone. Nonetheless, some people did manage to overcome the prejudices of the day, as evidenced by the
career of Martin de Porres.

Martin de Porres was born in Lima in 1579, the illegitimate son of Don Juan de Porres, a Spanish nobleman, and Ana Velázquez, a freed African slave from Panama. His father was disappointed that Martin had inherited his mother's dark skin and features, and so he delayed acknowledging paternity for eight years. Don Juan was still living with Ana, however, and she bore him a daughter named Juana two years after Martin was born. Ultimately, his father ended up abandoning the family while Martin was still a boy.

Martin thus grew up in poverty and because he was mixed-race he suffered much social stigma. He was able to attend school for two years and then at age twelve was apprenticed to a barber-surgeon, who taught him how to cut hair, bleed patients in keeping with current medical practice,[17] and prepare and administer medicines.

While still a boy, Martin began to develop an active prayer life, often spending much of the night praying and engaging in practices intended to subdue his bodily desires to devote himself more completely to God.

At age fifteen, he decided that he wanted to devote his life to the Catholic church, but Peru banned descendants of Africans and Indians from joining religious orders. Accordingly, Martin approached the Dominicans of the Convent of the Holy Rosary in Lima and asked to be taken as a servant.

---

17. Bleeding was a practice that came from ancient Greek medicine, which believed that disease was caused by an imbalance between the four humors in the body (blood, yellow bile, black bile, and phlegm). Bleeding was intended to restore the balance by removing excess blood from the body.

At first, he worked menial jobs and manual labor around the monastery. He was responsible for cleaning the rooms of the friars, and he was so careful and thorough about this that he was nicknamed "the saint of the broom." Meanwhile, he continued to develop his prayer life and spiritual practices and was particularly notable for his humility, which enabled him to ignore insults aimed at him for his mixed-race ancestry.

Martin's diligence and growing spirituality attracted the attention of his superiors in the convent. He was given more and more responsibilities, and his superiors decided to ignore the law and allow him to become a lay brother in the convent. He refused several times because he did not think he was worthy of the honor. Eventually, in 1603, his superiors ordered him to accept the position as a lay brother, and Martin reluctantly agreed.

Once he became a lay brother, many offices within the convent were opened to him. He continued to work in the kitchen, but not surprisingly, given his background, he became the convent's barber and began working in the infirmary. He was particularly skilled as a healer, and unlike many in his profession he treated everyone who came to him alike, whether rich or poor, Spanish or native, free or slave.

He was remarkably patient and giving in his work in the infirmary. At one point, he took in a beggar covered with ulcers and put him in his own bed to care for him. When one of the brothers in the convent rebuked him for this, he replied, "Compassion, my dear Brother, is preferable to cleanliness. Reflect that with a little soap I can easily clean my bed covers, but even with a torrent of tears I would never wash from my soul the stain that my harshness toward the unfortunate would create."[18]

At one point an epidemic broke out in Lima. Martin cared for the Holy Rosary's sick, but also began bringing people from the community into the convent for care. Eventually, the head of the Dominicans in Lima forbade him from bringing any more people in out of fear that the epidemic would spread to the brothers, so instead Martin began sending them to his sister's house in the countryside where he cared for them. One day he came across an Indian in the streets who had been stabbed. He brought the Indian into the convent and left him in his own room until he could arrange to send him to his sister's house. The convent's prior was angry about Martin's violation of the ban on bringing the infirm into the convent, but Martin replied, "Forgive my error, and please instruct me, for I did not know that the precept of obedience took precedence over that of charity."[19] After this response, the convent gave Martin permission to perform acts of mercy as his conscience dictated.

Martin's godly character, humility, and work in the infirmary soon led to stories of miracles. Many miraculous cures were attributed to him, sometimes administered simply by giving a patient a glass of water. It soon became rumored that

18. "Saint Martin de Porres, 1579-1639," Loyola Press, https://www.loyolapress.com/catholic-resources/saints/saints-stories-for-all-ages/saint-martin-de-porres/.
19. "St. Martin de Porres," Catholic Online, https://www.catholic.org/saints/saint.php?saint_id=306.

he could tell who would live and who would die, and that if he was very solicitous of you, you did not have long to live; conversely, if he largely ignored you, you would recover.

During the epidemic he is reported to have entered closed rooms of both novices and brothers without opening the doors; he simply appeared suddenly next to the brothers. Other stories tell of him bilocating, i.e., being in two places at the same time. In his prayers, people reported seeing him surrounded by light and, on at least one occasion, levitating.

Whatever we make of these reports, there can be no doubt of his compassion and skill as a healer. The stories themselves led to a number of very unusual opportunities for a mixed-race lay brother in a convent in this period. Many of the brothers and important members of the Lima community sought him out as a spiritual director and counselor, for example.

His reputation undoubtedly contributed to his effectiveness in other areas of ministry as well. For example, he was the convent's almoner. In this position, he was responsible for collecting alms to distribute to the poor and to support the convent. He collected enough money regularly that the convent was able to feed nearly 200 poor people per day plus take care of its own needs. He also raised a great deal of money to provide dowries for poor girls and to set up an orphanage for the poor in Lima's slums.

From his position as almoner, he soon became responsible for overseeing all the provisions of the monastery. At one point, when the convent was in financial difficulties, he urged them to sell him as a slave since he was just a poor mulatto who was the convent's property.

Martin also cared very deeply about animals. He would not eat meat, and he set up a shelter for stray cats and dogs at his sister's house. One amusing story often told about him concerned his love of animals and his responsibility to maintain the convent's clothing. Mice were eating the linen clothes in the wardrobe. Some of the brothers wanted to poison them, but Martin said they were just hungry. He caught one of the mice and told him to tell the other mice that he would feed them every day at the far end of the garden, but they had to stop eating the clothing. He put the mouse down, and that mouse and the others left the house and followed Martin into the garden. He fed them there each day, and there were no further problems with mice in the convent.

Because of his remarkable rapport with animals, Martin is often depicted with a broom and with a dog, cat, and mouse eating out of a common dish at his feet.

Despite taking care of the wardrobe, Martin's humility and frugality led him to wear his habits until they were falling apart. He did keep one fresh habit in his trunk, however, so it would be ready for his burial.

When Martin died, his funeral was more appropriate for a prominent public official than for a mixed-race lay brother. His body was laid out for people to pay their respects to him, and so many people snipped off parts of his habit to keep as relics that the habit had to be replaced three times. Father Caspar de Saldana, the prior of the monastery, conducted the funeral, and his pallbearers included the Viceroy of Peru, the Archbishop of Mexico, the Bishop of Cuzco, and John de Penafiel, a judge of the Royal Court in Lima, all his close friends. He was not buried with the lay brothers but with the priests, because everyone recognized he was worthy to be placed there. That evening, the archbishop commented, "Yes, this is the way saints should be honored."

Martin was considered a living saint during his lifetime, and many miraculous healings were attributed to him after his death. Yet the stigma of his mixed-race heritage and his African features followed him after his death. The church only officially recognized him as a saint in 1962, 323 years after his death. In contrast, his close friend Rose of Lima, a Dominican sister, was canonized in 1671, 54 years after her death. She, too, was mixed-race (her father was Spanish, her mother Creole), but she looked white. It is hard to escape the conclusion that Martin's race and appearance played an enormous part in the delay of his canonization.

Martin is now the patron saint of barbers (of course) and of social justice. His life is an example of genuine humility and compassion in the face of racial hostility and prejudice, and demonstrates that in the end, it is through practicing these qualities that we can overcome hatred and earn the respect that would otherwise be denied us out of bigotry or prejudice. In this way, we put into practice Paul's words, "Do not be overcome by evil, but overcome evil with good." (Rom. 12:21)

# MARTIN RINKART (1586-1649)
## *A Minister in a Time of War*

MARTIN RINKART WAS BORN ON APRIL 23, 1586, in Eilenburg, Saxony, a Lutheran state within the Holy Roman Empire. His father Georg was a cooper, a craftsman who made barrels. Martin learned Latin in his hometown, and then in 1601 became a foundation scholar and chorister at the St. Thomas School in Leipzig. His scholarship enabled him to go on to the University of Leipzig the following year where he began his studies of theology.

In 1610, Martin applied for the position of deacon in his hometown of Eilenburg. He went before the city council but was rejected for the position due to the opposition of the church's superintendent. His official reason for opposing Rinkart was that he was a better musician than theologian, though it seems likely he did not want a rival who was both from the town and thought for himself.

Rinkart then applied for a position as a teacher at the school in Eisleben, Luther's hometown. He was given the position and also acted as cantor for the Church of St. Nicholas in town. Within a year he was given the position of deacon in St. Anne's Church, also in Eisleben, which was the first church to officially adopt Protestantism about a century earlier. Then in 1613, he became pastor at Erdeborn and Lütjendorf near Eisleben.

Amid all his traveling and other duties, Rinkart found time to write. He wrote a series of seven dramas inspired by the hundred-year anniversary of the Reformation. Three were published in 1613, 1618, and 1623, and we know at least two were performed publicly. He was also named poet laureate in 1614 and wrote a large number of books as well as hymns and cantatas. Some of his books have been lost; others survive only in a single copy.

Rinkart completed his master's degree in theology in 1616, and then was finally offered the position of archdeacon in his hometown in 1617. He would spend the rest of his life there.

The year after he took his position in Eilenburg, the Thirty Years' War began. The Thirty Years' War is still remembered to this day as the most destructive war ever fought in Germany, and that includes World Wars I and II.[20] It featured

---

20. The World Wars resulted in more deaths in terms of raw numbers, but in terms of percentage of population, the Thirty Years' War killed a far greater percentage of the population. Further, the destruction of infrastructure, livestock, and the agricultural base condemned the entire region to over a century of recurring famines on top of the death toll during the war.

gunpowder armies much larger than those seen in the pre-gunpowder world, and these armies tried to live off the land by plundering since there were no systems in place to supply and pay them. You can't have multiple armies plundering a territory for thirty years without it doing an unbelievable and nearly irrecoverable amount of damage. The Holy Roman Empire (roughly modern Germany, Austria, the Czech Republic, and Slovakia) lost approximately one-third of its population during the war. It would not recover the lost population for a full century. Bohemia (half of the modern Czech Republic) may have lost as much as 70 percent of its population.

The war began as a conflict over religion in the nearby kingdom of Bohemia, but rapidly drew in almost all the countries of Europe. In principle, it was primarily a battle between the Catholic Holy Roman Emperor and his allies, and the Lutheran princes in the empire and their allies. In practice, it was far messier than that: for example, the Catholic emperor had a ruthless Protestant general named Albrecht von Wallenstein, and the Protestant princes were funded by Catholic France.

Along with Germany and Bohemia, the war also drew in the Swedes and Danes on the side of the German Lutherans, and Spain on the side of the emperor; the Dutch Republic was fighting for independence from Spain, so they were also drawn in; and France got involved militarily as a chance to take down Spain, an old rival ruled by the Habsburg family. The war was fought in Europe but it was also fought in the Americas and in the Indian Ocean as well.

Eilenburg was not immune to the effects of the war. It was a walled city, and so it became a place of refuge for people fleeing the violence. As troops came through the area, Rinkart and others were forced to quarter them in their houses, and their goods were regularly plundered by these soldiers. Not surprisingly, food was often scarce.

Then in 1637 plague arrived in the overcrowded city. Of the four clergy in Eilenburg, the superintendent fled the city, and the other two pastors soon succumbed to the disease. Rinkart was left alone to tend the sick and see to the burial of those who died. He performed up to fifty funerals per day, in all totaling over 4,480, including his wife's. Then the death toll got too high for individual funerals and trenches were dug for mass burials. The death toll was ultimately around 8,000.

After the plague came famine. Accounts from Eilenburg say that the famine was so severe that thirty or forty people would fight in the streets over a dead cat or crow. The burgomeister and Rinkart did their best to feed the people. Rinkart gave so much charity that he was forced to mortgage several years of his income just to feed and clothe his own children.

Then the Swedes came. Rinkart had saved the city once before from the Swedish army in 1637; now in the wake of the famine in 1639 they were back, demanding 30,000 florins as "tribute" from the city. Rinkart again went out to entreat them to lower their demands, but the Swedish general refused. Rinkart turned to the townspeople who had followed him out and said, "Come, my children, we can find no hearing, no mercy with men, let us take refuge with God."

He fell to his knees and began praying so earnestly that the general relented and asked for only 2,000 florins.

The war would drag on another eleven years. Rinkart's services had not made the town's leaders more grateful; they harassed him constantly, frequently about financial matters caused by his efforts to feed the starving people in the city. When peace finally came in 1648, Rinkart was exhausted and prematurely aged. He died the following year.

Given the difficulties of his life, it is surprising that the hymns that Rinkart penned were full of praise and trust in God even when they were speaking of the troubles that afflicted Germany. His best-known hymn, written c. 1636 in the middle of the war, was intended as a table prayer; we know it as the popular Thanksgiving hymn, "Now Thank We All Our God":

> Now thank we all our God, with heart and hands and
>     voices,
> Who wondrous things has done, in Whom this world
>     rejoices;
> Who from our mothers' arms has blessed us on our way
> With countless gifts of love, and still is ours today.
>
> O may this bounteous God through all our life be near us,
> With ever joyful hearts and blessèd peace to cheer us;
> And keep us in His grace, and guide us when perplexed;
> And free us from all ills, in this world and the next!
>
> All praise and thanks to God the Father now be given;

The Son and Him Who reigns with Them in highest
  Heaven;
The one eternal God, whom earth and Heaven adore;
For thus it was, is now, and shall be evermore.

Think about this hymn in the context of Rinkart's life. Perhaps the very difficulty of his circumstances led him to look to God alone for help, and yet he still found the faith to trust in God and to be grateful to him for his blessings. If in the midst of horrendously devastating war, plague, famine, and death, Rinkart could find the faith to sing his thanks to God, how much more should we, who are living in much better circumstances, rejoice in the goodness of God, who has blessed us so abundantly.

Rinkart was many things: an accomplished poet, musician, playwright, author, and pastor, but above all he was a man of extraordinary courage and faithfulness in horrific circumstances. Rather than complain about suffering, he endured it, stayed at his post, and remained thankful to God in faith for the abundant blessings given to us in Christ.

# MODERN TIMES

AMONG EUROPEAN HISTORIANS, THE
start of the French Revolution in 1789 marks the beginning of
the modern world. It is impossible in a short introduction to
cover even the most basic outline of the period, but a few comments will help put the following chapters in context. Within
the industrial world, the intelligentsia increasingly turned away
from Christianity and toward rationalism and scientism.[21] On
a global level, the nonindustrial world was increasingly dominated by the industrialized powers, mostly Europe and America. Ultimately, both of these trends contributed to the rise of
totalitarianism in Communist countries and Nazi Germany.

21. Scientism assumes that everything that happens has a purely material
cause and thus that science provides the best explanation for everything.
For example, love is nothing more than the feelings produced by the re-
lease of hormones triggered by your encounter(s) with another person.

But there were counter-movements to all of this. A burst of missionary activity around the world during the period spread Christianity as a global religion. While some missionaries were little more than tools of the colonial powers, others worked to modernize their mission fields to prepare them for independence. The spread of the Gospel led to indigenous Christians becoming political, cultural, and educational leaders fighting for human rights. Elsewhere, Quakers and British Evangelicals spearheaded the abolition movement in Britain and America, resulting in the end of legal slavery in much of the world for the first time in history. Many Blacks joined in this movement, not simply out of self-interest but as an expression of their Christian faith. More recently, Christians from around the world were inspired by their faith to work at great personal risk to save Jews from the Holocaust. The following chapters tell some of their stories.

# LEONHARD EULER (1707-1783)
## The Genius Mathematician

THE LATE 1600S THROUGH THE 1700S
saw European intellectuals turn away from the darkness
and superstition of the past in a movement that philosopher
Emanuel Kant dubbed the Enlightenment. Also known
as the Age of Reason, this period saw a growth in skepticism about Christianity, the rise of Deism and atheism, the
supremacy of reason over revelation, and a movement toward
irreligion, particularly among the intellectual elites.

Or so we are told in our history classes.

While there is an element of truth in this description of
intellectual life in the period, it ignores a number of important points. First, there were a number of counter-movements
within the churches that kept Christianity vital for many,

including among the elites. We see this in movements such as Jansenism among the Catholics, Pietism among the Lutherans, and the Evangelical revivals described in the last chapter.

Second, this view of the Enlightenment ignores the number of intellectual leaders who continued to hold to historic Christianity, such as Mersenne, Descartes, Pascal, Boyle, Newton, Hales.... Not all of these were completely orthodox in their views, but they were hardly Enlightenment rationalists when it came to religion. In fact, their religious faith helped impel them toward the kind of scientific advancement that is sometimes seen as the hallmark of Enlightenment thinking.

Perhaps the best example of an Enlightenment figure who made incredible contributions to the growth in knowledge of his era but who nonetheless maintained a robust Christian worldview is Leonhard Euler (pronounced roughly "oiler"). Although largely unknown outside of technical fields today, Euler was one of the greatest mathematical geniuses in history.

Leonhard was the son of Paul Euler, a pastor in the Reformed church in Basel, Switzerland. Shortly after his birth, the family moved to Riehen, a town in the Canton of Basel, but Leonhard returned to the capital city when he began his formal education. He matriculated at the University of Basel at age thirteen and completed his master's degree in philosophy in 1723 at the age of sixteen. His dissertation compared the philosophies of Descartes and Newton.

He continued his studies in theology, Greek, and Hebrew in preparation for becoming a pastor, but the direction of his life changed radically due to the influence of Johan

Bernoulli, the most famous mathematician in Europe and a family friend. Bernoulli was tutoring Leonhard in mathematics and realized that the boy had a remarkable gift. Bernoulli convinced Paul Euler that Leonhard was destined to become a great mathematician and so Leonhard changed the focus of his studies.

Euler completed a dissertation on the propagation of sound in 1726 and the following year took second place in a prestigious Paris Academy Prize Problem competition. (The subject was how to best place masts on a ship. He lost to Pierre Bouguer, who is known today as "the father of naval architecture.") In future years, Euler would go on to win the prize twelve times.

Meanwhile, Bernoulli's sons had taken positions at the St. Petersburg Academy of Sciences in Russia. Founded by Peter the Great (1672–1725), the academy's purpose was to help Russia catch up to the West in education and the sciences. Many European scholars spent time working there due to its large endowment.

When one of the Bernoulli brothers died of appendicitis in 1726, the surviving brother recommended Euler for a position. When a professorship at the University of Basel failed to materialize, Euler went to Russia. He initially worked in the medical department and was a medic to the Russian navy, but he rose rapidly through the ranks at the academy. He became a professor of physics in 1731, and when Daniel Bernoulli left the academy in 1733, Euler became head of the mathematics department.

In 1734, Euler married Katherina Gsell. They had thirteen children, though only five survived their childhood. The following year, Euler came down with a fever that left him nearly blind in his right eye. He blamed the loss of vision on the work he had been doing on cartography, but his vision in that eye continued to deteriorate over the next decades.

In 1741, growing xenophobia in Russia led Euler to accept a position at the Berlin Academy under Frederick the Great. In the twenty-five years he spent there, he published over 380 articles, along with important books on mathematical functions and on differential calculus.

Frederick also asked Euler to mentor his niece, the Princess of Anhalt Dessau. Euler wrote her over 230 letters, which were later compiled into a bestselling book entitled *Letters of Euler on Different Subjects in Natural Philosophy Addressed to a German Princess*. These letters deal not just with science and philosophy but also address religious issues and reveal much of Euler's personality and beliefs.

Unfortunately, Euler's faith and his conservative, hardworking lifestyle did not sit well with the atmosphere at Frederick's court, particularly after the arrival of Voltaire, the anti-Christian French satirist and *philosophe*. The situation in Russia had stabilized under Catherine the Great, so in 1761 Euler accepted an invitation to return to the St. Petersburg Academy of Sciences.

Five years later, Euler was diagnosed with a cataract in his left eye. Within a few weeks of its diagnosis, he was completely blind. This would normally have ended his career, but Euler became even more productive in some areas than he had been before. How could he do this?

Euler had a number of qualities that make this feat at least somewhat understandable. His ability to concentrate was legendary: according to Condorcet, two of his students had summed seventeen terms in a complicated infinite series but could not agree on the fifteenth decimal point; Euler settled the argument by doing the calculation in his head and telling them the result. He was immune to distraction, frequently writing his treatises with his children playing at his feet. He also had a prodigious capacity for hard work, for example producing roughly one mathematical treatise a week for an entire year in 1775. Further, he had a photographic memory: he could recite Virgil's *Aeneid* verbatim and could even tell his audience the first and last lines from any page of the edition he had learned.

By the end of his life, Euler had produced 886 papers and books filling roughly ninety volumes, making him the most productive mathematician in history with the possible exception of Paul Erdös (1913–1996). In fact, the last phase of his life was so prolific that the St. Petersburg Academy did not complete publication of his papers until thirty years after his death.

It is difficult for a non-mathematician to understand or describe Euler's work. The best way to describe it is to simply note the range of his work. In mathematics, Euler developed many of the symbols for advanced calculations that are still in use today. He did work in infinitesimal calculus, geometry, trigonometry, algebra, graph theory, and applied mathematics. He also created the field of analytical number theory, uniting number theory and analytical mathematics for the first time.

He also worked in physics, astronomy, acoustics, and optics. He returned to the ancient liberal arts tradition and tried to reunite music and mathematics (with only limited success: his work was too mathematical for musicians and too musical for mathematicians). And he also introduced some significant advancements in logic.

All of this barely scratches the surface of Euler's work. To put it in perspective, there is a Wikipedia entry entitled "List of Things Named after Leonhard Euler" that includes seventy-eight items derived from his work, plus another nine named in honor of him. The entry notes that there is a joke among mathematicians and physicists that to avoid naming everything after him, discoveries and theorems are named after the first person *after* Euler to discover them.

Even with this prodigious output in mathematics and physics, Euler never left behind the theological commitments and interests of his youth. Like many Christian scholars of the time, he entered into the debates against the more anti-religious thinkers of his day. We see this in both his letters to Frederick the Great's niece and in his *Rettung der Göttlichen Offenbahrung Gegen die Einwürfe der Freygeister* (*Defense of the Divine Revelation against the Objections of the Freethinkers*), a defense of biblical inspiration.

At times his mathematical work intersected with his philosophical and theological ideas. For example, following early Christian natural philosophers, he insisted that knowledge was based in part on precise quantitative laws, so that he dismissed philosophical systems that could not provide these laws as "heathen and atheistic."

More often, however, his mathematical work was an expression of his deep faith as a Christian who recognized that Jesus as the *logos* was the sum of all knowledge and truth. All his work was thus an expression of his worldview that recognized that every area of life was worth exploring as an act of worship and service of God. In an age where skepticism and unbelief were on the rise, Euler stood firm in his convictions and defended the faith with vigor, all the while studying mathematics and physics as branches of natural philosophy, anchored in the *logos*, and revealing something of the mind of God.

# OLAUDAH EQUIANO

## (C. 1745-1797)

### *The Slave Who Fought for Abolition*

WHEN WE THINK OF THE MOVEMENT to abolish slavery, we usually think of people like William Wilberforce or Thomas Clarkson in England, or Harriet Beecher Stowe, Harriet Tubman, or Frederick Douglass in America. None of these, however, were born in Africa, enslaved, and suffered the horrors of the "Middle Passage" across the Atlantic. One important, though largely forgotten, abolitionist did: Olaudah Equiano, also known as Gustavus Vassa.

Equiano was born in Eboe, a village far from the coast in modern Nigeria. At age eleven, while the adults in his village were working, slave raiders captured him and his sister and took them away. The siblings were separated, and aside from a brief meeting before being transported from Africa, they never saw each other again.

Olaudah was renamed Michael and shipped to Barbados in the West Indies on a ship that carried 245 slaves, and from there he and a few others were sent to the English colony in Virginia. In Virginia, his original owner called him Jacob and used him as a domestic slave. Soon, he was sold to an English naval lieutenant named Michael Pascal, who renamed him Gustavus Vassa after the new king of Sweden. He objected to the new name at first, which earned him a beating, but eventually he gave in. He continued to use the name Gustavus Vassa for the rest of his life.

As the slave of a naval officer, Equiano was trained in seamanship and assisted the crew during the naval battles of the Seven Years' War (known in America as the French and Indian War) in both Canada and the Mediterranean. Pascal was impressed with Equiano, so he sent him to his sister-in-law in England to allow him to attend school. While there, he converted to Christianity (at least formally) and was baptized.

When the war ended in 1763, Equiano was denied a share of the prize money earned by the crew, and Pascal reneged on his promise to free him. Instead, he sold him to James Doran, a merchant, with instructions to sell him to the best master he could since Equiano was "a very deserving boy." Doran took him to the Caribbean, where he was sold to Robert King, a Quaker merchant from Philadelphia.

Quakers were leaders in the abolition movement; in fact, under the influence of the Quaker John Woolman slavery was in severe decline in Pennsylvania. It may seem odd, then, that a Quaker merchant should purchase Equiano, but King had no intention of keeping him a slave. King informed Equiano that he was free to engage in trade while he worked with him, and that when he could reimburse King for his purchase price, he would be freed. Equiano sold small items such as glass tumblers and fruit in the trips King took between Georgia and the Caribbean and worked with King to improve his reading and writing.

In 1766, he had earned enough money to purchase his freedom. Although King wanted Equiano to continue working with him as a business partner, Equiano decided against it: he had been nearly kidnapped and re-enslaved in Georgia, so he decided it was safer for him to get out of the British colonies.

Equiano traveled to London, where he was finally paid his wages by the Royal Navy (though still denied his prize money from Pascal). He tried to make a living as a hairdresser, but this didn't pay well so he returned to sea. He undertook several very pleasant voyages around the Mediterranean and one to the Caribbean before joining a polar expedition in an unsuccessful attempt to find the Northwest Passage (i.e., a route north of Canada that would enable a ship to sail between the Atlantic and Pacific Oceans). A young midshipman named Horatio Nelson was on this expedition. Nelson would later become famous as the admiral who defeated the French at the Battle of the Nile and at Trafalgar.

In 1763, after the polar expedition, Equiano returned to London where he found out that one of his friends, a freed slave named John Annis, had been re-enslaved by his former owner in violation of the law. Equiano got in touch with Granville Sharp, the most prominent abolitionist in England, and together they tried unsuccessfully to have Annis freed. Although he was not yet fully engaged in the abolitionist cause, Equiano's contacts with Sharp would be very important in future years.

At about this time, Equiano had what he considered the most important experience of his life while on a voyage to Spain: a heartfelt conversion to Christianity. He tells us he saw "bright beams of heavenly light" and was "born again." He joined the Methodists and became part of the broader British Evangelical community.

In the eighteenth century, the church of England looked askance at people who took their faith too seriously. You were expected to be baptized, attend church on Sundays and holy days, get confirmed and married in the church, and when you died get buried in the churchyard, and not much else. Too much interest in religion would lead to accusations of "enthusiasm," roughly like being called a "holy roller" or fanatic in America today. Yet the 1700s saw a series of revivals in the British Isles and their colonies in America. These included Calvinist revivals in Wales, the Methodist revivals in both their Calvinist and Arminian forms, and the First Great Awakening in America. Across the board, the British Evangelicals who came out of these revivals shared four characteristics: they had a strong commitment to the Bible; they believed in the necessity of conversion; they believed that true faith required transformation of life; and they believed they needed to transform society in alignment with the Gospel. Not surprisingly, one of their first targets was the abolition of slavery.

In 1775, Equiano was involved in setting up a "plantation" (i.e., a colony) in Central America. He signed up as a Christian missionary but was heavily involved in planning the colony, including bringing in African slaves. At this time, the anti-slavery movement had yet to get organized, and most people believed that slavery was simply a part of life; that did not mean, however, that slaves should be mistreated. Equiano thus worked to see that slaves were well treated in the colony, but events pushed him to become a full-fledged abolitionist: he was again cheated out of his money, and was nearly re-enslaved, only barely escaping by canoe from his captor.

Equiano thus returned to London, where for seven years he worked as a servant and became increasingly involved in the abolitionist cause. Among other things, he fed information on the slave trade to Granville Sharp and alerted him to the Zong Massacre, when the crew of a British slave ship that was running low on drinking water due to navigational errors threw 142 slaves off the ship to drown.

Equiano also became acutely aware of the problem of poor Africans begging on the streets of London, and with other abolitionists he advocated a program to return them to Africa. He was involved in the establishment of the colony of Sierra Leone, becoming the first black civil servant in British history. He quickly recognized that others involved in the project were lining their own pockets with money needed to make the colony work, and when he protested he lost his job.

It turns out he was right: only sixty of the people shipped to the colony survived its first four years, largely because they lacked the means to feed themselves due to the graft of the colonial administrators.

Equiano's next project was writing his autobiography, *The Interesting Narrative of the Life of Olaudah Equiano, or Gustavus Vassa, the African* (1789). There had been a few narratives of slaves' lives published at this point, though only one had been actually written by a former slave rather than by a white author who transcribed the words.

Equiano's was the first extensive book to document the life of a slave, and the first self-published autobiography of a former slave. He funded the book via subscriptions from a number of very influential people, including eight dukes and the Prince of Wales.

It is hard to overstate the importance of this book to the abolitionist cause. It described in detail the horrors of the slave trade and the abuse and torture of slaves in the British colonies and presented a number of both religious and economic arguments for the abolition of slavery. Further, the book's clear, elegant, and powerful prose implicitly made the broader point that given the opportunity to learn, Africans were every bit the equal of Europeans. The book thus became an important piece of the abolitionists' campaign to alert Britain to the immorality of the slave trade and to sway public opinion away from its unthinking support of slavery.

*The Interesting Narrative* also made Equiano a lot of money, freeing him up to spend the 1790s traveling to promote the book and in the process the cause of abolition. He worked very closely with parliamentarian William Wilberforce and the Clapham Circle that formed around him in their efforts to build public support for abolition. He was also involved in other social organizations, including the London Corresponding Society, which advocated extending the franchise to working-class men; the Sierra Leone Company to continue assisting the colony; and the London Missionary Society, a non-denominational Christian mission agency. Like Wilberforce, his Christian commitments led him to work not just on the abolition of slavery but on other social causes as well.

In 1792, he also found time to marry Susannah Cullen, an English woman from Cambridgeshire. They had two daughters, one of whom survived to inherit a sizable sum from her father's estate.

Equiano died in 1797, a year after his wife, ten years before the abolition of the slave trade, and thirty-six years before slavery itself was abolished in the British Empire. Nonetheless, his efforts were vitally important for eradicating this great evil in the empire and helped set the groundwork for abolition in the United States as well.

It is easy to forget that Christianity had opposed slavery for centuries before the abolition movement. Thomas Aquinas, for example, saw slavery as a violation of natural law and thus a sin, and four separate Renaissance popes condemned the Atlantic slave trade. The Catholic countries of Portugal and Spain ignored the popes, and when the English took over the slave trade in 1715, they were mired in a formalistic religion that had a form of godliness but denied the power thereof. It was the Quakers and Evangelicals who recognized the slave trade and built the movement to bring it to an end. It is ironic and unfortunate that the work of an African Christian in helping to end the African slave trade has been largely forgotten in most discussions of the abolitionist movement.

# BENJAMIN RUSH (1745-1813)
## Christian Founding Father and Educator

ALTHOUGH SCHOLARS AND TEACH-
ers in America were aware of and interacted with Enlightenment ideas emanating from Europe, they retained much
more of historic Christian thought than is often recognized.
In New England, this was rooted in the Puritanism of the
region's founders; especially in the northern colonies, the
Great Awakening was also an important element in shaping
the mindset of the colonies.

To take just two examples, the Puritans were Calvinists
who accepted the idea of total depravity, that is, that every
aspect of our being is infected by sin; they further accepted
the Augustinian idea of original sin that said that everyone
without exception is corrupt and corruptible. The practical

upshot of this is that government officials, who were themselves subject to original sin and total depravity, could not be trusted with unlimited power.

The revivalists in the Great Awakening argued that a plowboy who had been converted was the spiritual superior of a bishop who had not had a conversion experience. This undermined the hierarchical assumptions that were embedded in European society and contributed tremendously to the republican sentiments leading up to the American Revolution. And when combined with the influence of Calvinism, it led to the conclusion that it was up to the people to oversee their governors and make sure their laws aligned with truth as revealed in Scripture. And this required education, first among the pastorate, then among the people.

As had been the case in Europe, schools in the American colonies were founded almost entirely by churches or other religious organizations. This is most obvious at the university level: Harvard, William and Mary, Yale, Princeton, Brown, all were founded as religious institutions.

But in addition to higher education, primary schools were also set up to teach the Bible. There were several reasons for this. As we have seen, Christians have always believed in the importance of the life of the mind, and thus have always valued education. Especially in the wake of the Reformation, they also believed that studying the Bible was essential for active citizens in a republic. For example, in the New England colonies, public schools emphasized biblical studies so that the people could test any proposed laws against scriptural standards to prevent abuse of power by their leaders.

More broadly, Protestants maintained that developing a biblical worldview was essential to producing a prosperous and successful society. Though no one argued that the Bible was all anyone needed to study, they did believe that the Bible provided an essential framework for studying any discipline, and that its teachings about how to live were essential for civic and personal virtue.

These ideas continued to influence American society through the Revolution into the Early Republic, including the signers of the Declaration of Independence. One example is Benjamin Rush.

Rush was one of seven children born to John and Susanna Rush in the Township of Byberry outside of Philadelphia. His father died when he was five, and at eight he was sent to live with relatives. He studied at a school directed by Rev. Samuel Finley in Nottingham, Pennsylvania, and then at the College of New Jersey (now Princeton University) at age ten. He completed his degree in 1760 at the age of fifteen.

Rush then began training with John Redman, a physician in Philadelphia. With Redman's support, Rush moved to the University of Edinburgh, where he received his medical degree. After practicing medicine for a time in Britain, in 1769 he returned to the colonies. At the age of twenty-four, he opened a medical practice in Philadelphia and was named chemistry professor at the College of Philadelphia (now the University of Pennsylvania). During this period, he wrote the first textbook on chemistry published in America and produced several treatises on medical education.

Along with his medical work, Rush was an ardent patriot. He wrote numerous patriotic essays, and Thomas Paine even consulted with him when he wrote *Common Sense*, one of the most influential pro-independence pamphlets of the era. Rush was appointed to the Continental Congress and became a signatory of the Declaration of Independence. Shortly thereafter, he became a surgeon general in the Continental Army, though a year later he resigned due to conflicts with other physicians in the military. He also was not a fan of George Washington and called for his removal, an action that he later regretted. After the Revolution, Rush continued his work in politics, notably as part of the Pennsylvania convention that ratified the US Constitution.

Rush also continued his medical career after the war. He joined the staff of Pennsylvania Hospital and taught medical theory and clinical practice at the University of Pennsylvania. Over his career, he educated over 300 physicians. He also founded Dickinson College, a liberal arts college in Carlisle, Pennsylvania.

One significant area of study for Rush was the treatment of mental illness. He argued that the mentally ill shouldn't be chained up in dungeons but brought into normal hospital settings. He also believed that giving them productive work could aid in their recovery. Both of these proved to be successful strategies in treating many of his patients.

Along with his medical work, Rush was active in social reform. He was a founding member of the Philadelphia Society for Alleviating the Miseries of Public Prisons (the Pennsylvania Prison Society today). He was also an ardent abolitionist, writing pamphlets against the institution of slavery in 1773 and joining abolitionist societies. He very specifically argued on scientific grounds that blacks were in no way inferior to whites.

This is quite a resume, but it is important to realize that all of these activities were very directly informed by Rush's faith. His stands on mental health, prisons, and slavery all came from his understanding that each person is made in the image of God and therefore deserves to be treated with dignity and respect. His observations on the importance of work for our well-being confirmed ideas contained within the biblical worldview.

His stand on abolition had been the historical position of the church and in his day was being advanced by Evangelicals (among others) in Britain and America. He was so concerned with the well-being of the black population that he acted as an advisor to Richard Allen in the founding of the African Methodist Episcopal Church and lent it his public support.

Rush's views on politics were similarly drawn from the Christian tradition. His ideas on unalienable rights can be traced through John Locke all the way back to medieval scholastic theologians, and his ideas of liberty and tyranny likewise trace through Locke to Protestant resistance theory developed in response to persecution in the sixteenth century.

Even more, the entire spirit of the Gospel led Rush to his political views. He believed that Christians had to be republicans because God made all people equal; there is no room for a "divine right of kings" in Christianity. Further, Christians make the best citizens of a republic since the very virtues that allow a republic to succeed are those taught by the Gospel.

As a result, Rush believed firmly that a Christian education was essential to the nation's success and so he championed education on all levels. Along with his work at the collegiate level, he is considered the father of American public education and was a major supporter of the American Sunday School Union. But not any education would do: it needed to be firmly grounded in Scripture if it was to produce the kind of citizen that would lead to a prosperous society. Like Martin Luther,[22] he believed that an education without a moral foundation would do more harm than good.

To put it differently, Rush believed that education was vitally important to produce a virtuous society, but that education needed to be based in Scripture. In fact, teaching the Bible was not just about salvation but contributed to both personal and societal well-being.

This is an attitude that can be found throughout church history: because the biblical worldview is true, understanding and following it produces good results for both the individual and society and in the end also leads to Heaven. Christianity is thus not an otherworldly religion. Rather, it believes in the goodness of this world and works to repair what is wrong

---

22. Luther commented, "I am much afraid that the schools will prove the very gates of hell, unless they diligently labor in explaining the Holy Scriptures, and engraving them in the hearts of youth. I advise no one to place his child where the scriptures do not reign paramount. Every institution in which means are not unceasingly occupied with the Word of God must be corrupt." *Address to the Christian Nobility of the German Nation.*

here, not just to prepare for Heaven. And that process begins with education.

Rush was not alone here. While the American founders were influenced to a greater or lesser extent by Enlightenment thought, Christianity was an important influence on all of them as well. Calvinism and British Evangelicalism shaped not only their religious lives but their vision of government and the things that are necessary for human flourishing. We ignore these elements of their thought today at the peril of our republic and our liberty.

# WILLIAM CAREY (1761–1834)
## *The Evangelist of India*

THE STEREOTYPE MANY PEOPLE HOLD of missionaries is that they were agents of Western imperialism engaged in cultural genocide and the oppression of native peoples. And there were times when this did indeed happen, but more often missions were done with the intent of both bringing salvation and improving the lives of native people, often in opposition to imperialist agendas. Missions to India are a case in point.

In the 1700s, the Indian subcontinent was divided into a large number of independent states. European countries had established colonies at a number of locations around the region, but by far the most important colonial power was not a nation but a company.

The British East India Company had been granted a royal monopoly to trade in the "East Indies" (later expanded to include virtually all of Asia) in 1600. In 1612, the Mughal emperor allowed them to set up business in Gujrat. Over the rest of the century the company expanded to become arguably the most important power in the subcontinent, operating across the boundaries of kingdoms and even setting up its own army to defend its interests. In the second half of the eighteenth century, the company began to rule much of India outright in what became known as the *Raj*.

The company was not particularly concerned about religious or educational matters; in fact, keeping the Indian peoples divided by religion, ethnicity, language, and caste suited their purposes of maximizing profits. Introducing Christian missionaries into India could prove to be disruptive, and so the company did not allow them into its territories.

Missions to India opened up largely due to the work of Charles Grant. Grant had gone to India as part of the company's military but rose through the ranks to be put in charge of trade in Bengal and then to become part of the company's board of trade. After losing two children to smallpox, Grant experienced a religious conversion. As a result, he began to see India as desperately in need of the kind of social and moral reform that Christianity could bring, including an end to infanticide, burning widows and lepers, and a host of other social ills.

Grant returned to England and became a member of Parliament. He joined the Clapham sect with William Wilberforce, and together they worked in Parliament to force the

East India Company to accept missionaries in India as a condition for the renewal of the company charter.

The most important missionary to go to India in the wake of this decision was William Carey. The son of weavers, Carey was apprenticed to a cobbler and eventually inherited a shoemaking business from his master. As an apprentice, Carey taught himself Latin and, with the help of a local vicar, Greek; as a shoemaker he learned Hebrew, Italian, French, and Dutch.

A fellow apprentice influenced Carey to become a Dissenter from the church of England. He eventually became a Particular Baptist and, influenced by the writings of Jonathan Edwards, picked up a passion for missions. In 1789, Carey became a full-time pastor and worked very hard to overcome the hyper-Calvinism of the Particular Baptists. "Particular" (as opposed to "General") Baptists focused on the idea that God predestined particular people to salvation, and thus that we had little to do with bringing people to faith. It was completely the work of God. As a result, the Particular Baptists were very resistant to the idea of missions and evangelism. In 1792, he spearheaded the founding of the Particular Baptist Society for the Propagation of the Gospel amongst the Heathen (later called the Baptist Missionary Society). The following year he left England for India. Opposition from the British East India Company delayed his arrival in India; he only made it there by sailing on a Danish vessel to Denmark's colony in India.

It is impossible in a brief article to even begin to cover all aspects of the work of Carey and his companions. Just looking at Carey himself, he made important contributions to botanical knowledge, as well as promoting agriculture and forestry in India. He taught astronomy in an effort to move India beyond the fatalism found in astrology. He fought for moral reforms such as women's rights, including education for girls and an end to sati (burning widows on their husbands' funeral pyres), medical treatment for lepers, and the abolition of the caste system among converts to Christianity. He brought the steam engine to India and encouraged local blacksmiths to copy it. He set up the first banking system in India as well.

Impressive though this list is, all of these accomplishments fade to insignificance compared to Carey's multifaceted work in education. He studied and mastered several Indian languages and translated classical Indian literature for the first time into English. He eventually became a professor of Bengali, Sanskrit, and Marathi at Fort William College in Calcutta. His studies enabled him to produce the first Sanskrit dictionary, opening the language to European scholars.

Carey's work was not simply scholarly, however. He brought the first printing press to India and developed typefaces for Indian languages. From there, he supervised the translation of all or part of the Bible into forty-four different Indian languages. In the process, he also established the first newspaper in Asia and the first lending libraries in India using books imported from England.

With his companions Joshua Marshman and William Ward, Carey began the process of learning the hundreds of dialects spoken in India and reducing them to seventy-three written languages, complete with grammars and dictionaries. His work enabled Bengali to emerge as the major literary language of India. As a result, Carey is often considered the father of the Indian Renaissance in the nineteenth and twentieth centuries. Other missionaries such as John Borthwick Gilchrist (1759–1841) virtually created modern Hindi and Urdu out of the jumble of dialects of Hindustani.

Carey wasn't only involved with printing, however. He set up schools for all castes, breaking the Brahmin monopoly on learning, and was instrumental in founding the first college in Asia at Serampore. The language of the college was Bengali: Indian families wanted their children to learn just enough English to get jobs, but no more, and Carey was more interested in producing educated Indians than English-speaking workers for the company.

And that goal, which was very much in keeping with the attitudes of the English missionaries, set them at odds with the company. Even though the company had to accept the missionaries, they were never happy about having them in India. It was in the company's interests to preserve the status quo in the subcontinent, and they feared the disruption Christian conversions would cause. But the attitude of the missionaries toward the Indians and the company was an even more serious threat to the *Raj*.

Carey and the other missionaries with him set out to improve the lives of the Indian people comprehensively: they worked to end social practices that destroyed lives, brought science, technology, and economic development, and provided education in Western learning, all of which they saw as flowing out of their Christian faith. And they knew that over time, this would transform India.

In other words, rather than being a tool of the colonial powers, the missionaries saw their responsibility as empowering the Indian people. Later missionaries and their supporters such as Charles Trevelyan (1807–1886) and Lord Macauley (1800–1859) were very explicit that with education and cultural reform, the Indian people would develop institutions of self-government and would become independent of Britain and the company. Much as American Founding Father Benjamin Rush had seen republican self-government as an outworking of biblical principles, so Carey and the other missionaries to India saw their work in promoting the biblical worldview as leading to the emergence of India as a modern, self-governing nation.

Carey did all of this despite enormous setbacks. A fire destroyed much of his print shop, including priceless manuscripts of translations and other work that he was never able to recreate. Beyond this, his family life suffered from his work. His first wife, Dorothy, was an English peasant nowhere near his level intellectually and ill-prepared for the culture shock that awaited her in India. When their son Peter died of dysentery, she had a nervous breakdown and suffered from serious mental illness for the rest of her life. William Carey also seems to have seriously neglected his other sons, giving them neither the education nor the discipline that they needed, according to a missionary who joined the team later. For all his remarkable success as a mission leader, he failed his family in many ways.

Carey is considered the father of modern missions; his linguistic and educational work, inspired by his biblical worldview, made him also the father of the Indian Renaissance in the nineteenth and twentieth centuries. For Carey, education in all subjects was inseparable from true Christianity since Christianity is a comprehensive worldview that is vitally concerned with all of life. As a result of this broad vision of the Gospel, Carey helped lay the groundwork for modern India.

# KRISHNA MOHAN
# BANNERJEE (1813-1885)
### *Indian Educator and Apologist*

INDIA IN THE NINETEENTH CENTURY
was coming to grips with the modern world thanks to its
exposure to England through the British East India Company and through the work of missionaries such as William
Carey. Some of the most creative interaction with Western
culture occurred in Bengal, due in part to Carey's work in
creating a unified Bengal language and in opposing practices
such as sati.

One of the most important figures in the development
of Western education in Bengal was David Hare (1775–
1842). Hare was a watchmaker from Scotland who moved
to India. He does not seem to have had any particular faith

commitments, but he was very concerned about social welfare in Bengal and began several very important schools in the area featuring English education.

Krishna Mohan Bannerjee was born in Bengal in 1813 as Bengali and English culture were beginning to interact more actively. He attended the School Society Institution started by David Hare in Kalitala in 1819. Hare quickly recognized the boy's talent and took him to his school in Pataldanga, later known as Hare School.

Bannerjee excelled in his studies and earned a scholarship to the newly founded Hindu College (now Presidency University) in Calcutta. This school had been established by a number of prominent English and Indian leaders, including Raja Ram Mohan Roy. Roy has been called the "Father of the Bengal Renaissance," as well as the "Maker of Modern India" and the "Father of Modern India." Among other things, Roy founded *Brahmo Samaj*, a monotheistic reform movement in Hinduism that worked to eliminate idolatry, sati, and polygamy, and to bring in ethical ideas drawn from the Judeo-Christian tradition and from Islam. Significantly, some Indian intellectuals were just as critical about elements of Hindu culture as the colonizers were.

The headmaster of Hindu College was Henry Louis Vivian Derozio. Although of mixed Portuguese descent, Derozio considered himself a Bengali. He was something of a radical and was one of the first people to spread Western learning and science among the young men of Bengal. He advocated free discussion and debate on any and every issue. His students took to calling themselves "Derozians," though they were known more generally as the Young Bengals.

Bannerjee thrived at Hindu College and was profoundly influenced by Derozio. He stayed at his grandfather's house in Calcutta, which also became a meeting place for the Young Bengals.

Perhaps under the influence of the freethinking Derozio, or perhaps in the kind of prank college students today might do, one day Bannerjee and other Young Bengals ate bread and meat prepared by a Muslim, which was taboo to upper-caste Hindus. They followed up by throwing the bones into a neighbor's yard while chanting, "Cow meat! Cow meat!" This caused a near riot, and his grandfather had to throw him out of the house.

Bannerjee moved in with friends and continued his studies. When his father died of cholera in 1828, he had to support himself with manual labor, but he still excelled in his examinations at the school. When he graduated from the Hindu College in 1829, he got a job teaching at David Hare's Pataldanga school.

The following year, Scottish missionary Dr. Alexander Duff arrived in Calcutta. Noticing that Christian missions in India had only reached the lower castes, Duff proposed a new missions strategy: he offered education in English in the sciences and in biblical studies, with the goal of helping upper-caste Hindu students to see the contradictions in their beliefs and to move them toward Christianity. Like many others, Duff connected Western learning and success with Christianity, and he believed that making Western learning and the Bible available would inevitably lead to conversions.

Bannerjee began attending Duff's lectures and even visiting his house for serious discussions about religion and philosophy. In 1832, Bannerjee converted to Christianity, probably as a result of his relationship with Duff. The conversion cost Bannerjee: Hare fired him from the school, and his wife was forced to return to her father's home. (She would return to him later.) There was also a firestorm in the local press about the Hindu College, ironically with the atheist Derozio being blamed for Bannerjee's conversion. The popular headmaster was thus forced out.

Even prior to his conversion, Bannerjee had become increasingly critical of some aspects of Hinduism. He wrote a play in 1831 entitled *The Persecuted, or, Dramatic Scenes Illustrative of the Present State of Hindoo Society in Calcutta* that was focused on exposing social injustices in Indian society. He also began a journal called *The Inquirer* that same year.

After his conversion, Bannerjee became the headmaster of the Church Missionary Society School. He also studied theology at Bishop's College, and when he graduated in 1839 he became the first Indian to be ordained a priest in the Anglican church in Bengal.

His education made Bannerjee the foremost Indian apologist of his day. Prior to 1865, he followed the lead of Duff and other missionaries in seeing Hinduism as nothing but superstition and idolatry that needed to be destroyed. Accordingly, he worked to demonstrate the errors and weaknesses of Hindu philosophy, to disprove the divine origin of the Vedas, and to identify Hinduism with Buddhism and therefore with atheism.

After 1865, however, he changed his entire approach to apologetics. He began to argue that Christianity was actually the fulfillment of Hinduism. He noted that sacrifice was the most important ritual in the earliest forms of Hinduism. Further, he showed from the Vedas, the Upanishads, and other Hindu writings that Prajapati, the Lord and Supporter of Creation, sacrificed himself to save humanity and, to do so, took on a mortal body. He was thus, in the words of Bannerjee, "half human and half divine." All of this, Bannerjee argued, prefigured Jesus' incarnation and sacrifice on the cross.

Bannerjee's efforts to find a doorway from Hinduism to Christianity grew out of his love of his country and his culture. For all of his interest in Western learning, he was very proud of India and of Bengal. He wanted to reconcile Christianity and modern education with Indian culture. In keeping with this goal, he became heavily involved in a wide range of organizations in Bengal. These included the Society for the Acquisition of General Knowledge, the Bethune Society, the Calcutta Text Book Society, the Bengal Social Science Association, the Family Literary Club, the Asiatic Society of Bengal, the Index Association, the Bible Association, and Calcutta University, the British India Association, the India League, and the Indian Association.

He was also involved in social reform. He opposed the caste system, polygamy, idolatry, the sale of girls into marriage, and sati; he also supported the education of women and believed that it was the yardstick that measured the social progress of a country.

He believed that his countrymen should be educated in English, Sanskrit, and Bengali. In particular, at a time when the vernacular was held in very low regard, he advocated for Bengali and wrote a number of works on a variety of subjects in the language. Ultimately, his work in literature and higher education was rewarded with an honorary Doctor of Law degree from Calcutta University in 1876. In 1885, the British government awarded him the rank of Companion of the Indian Empire.

Bannerjee's work led many to Christ. Among others, he is responsible for converting Lal Behari Dey, a journalist and writer who became a minister of the Gospel, professor of English and philosophy, and social reformer concerned about the plight of the poor. Another of his converts was Gnanendra Mohan Tagore, the first Asian called to the bar in England. He also influenced the conversion of Michael Madhusudan Dutt, one of the foremost Bengali poets and the creator of the Bengali sonnet.

Beyond his work as an evangelist and apologist, Bannerjee was also a critically important figure in the Bengal Renaissance, in bringing modern ideas of scholarship and social justice to India, and in developing an approach to Christianity that honored Indian culture but was firmly anchored in the British Evangelical tradition. He was a remarkable example of contextualizing the Gospel to India while applying the biblical worldview to all areas of life.

# OCTAVIUS VALENTINE
## CATTO (1839-1871)
### *Free Black Champion of Slaves*

WHEN WE THINK OF RACE RELATIONS in the era of the Civil War, we naturally think about slavery; if we take it beyond the Civil War, we might remember the Fifteenth Amendment, which gave Blacks the right to vote. But we often forget that even in states like Pennsylvania, which had long outlawed slavery, racism extended far beyond just these issues. We also forget that free Blacks in the North were active in both the abolitionist cause and in fighting for civil rights. Few were more effective than the now largely forgotten Octavius Valentine Catto.

Octavius Valentine Catto was born of mixed-race parents in slave-holding South Carolina. His mother, Sarah Isabella

Cain, was a free woman from the prominent mixed-race DeReef family; since in America a man's status at birth came from his mother, Octavius was born free. His father, William T. Catto, was a freed slave who had become a Presbyterian minister.

William Catto moved the family out of Charleston, South Carolina, to Philadelphia, a city that had long been opposed to slavery and where free blacks had far more opportunities than they had in the south.

Octavius began his education in segregated schools in Philadelphia, though he spent some time in the otherwise all-white Allentown Academy in Allentown, New Jersey. In 1854, he returned to Philadelphia where he attended the Institute for Colored Youth (ICY) run by the Quakers (later renamed Cheyney University, the country's first historically black institution of higher education). The ICY had been founded as a trade school but had changed its curriculum to liberal arts and classics by the time Catto arrived. Catto graduated from the ICY in 1858, then spent a year in advanced studies under a black scholar in Washington, DC. He returned to Philadelphia in 1859, where he was appointed as a teacher of English and mathematics at the ICY by its principal, Ebenezer Bassett, an African American graduate of Yale and future ambassador to Haiti.

Along with teaching at the ICY, Catto was involved in the Banneker Institute, an African American scholarly organization. He was also elected to the Franklin Institute of Science over strenuous opposition by a significant percentage of its white members.

During this period Catto also became an activist on racial issues. He argued against the common practice of appointing incompetent or racist white teachers to black schools and pointed out the difficulties even highly qualified blacks had in finding jobs. He also began agitating for abolition and for voting rights for blacks, a cause that he would continue to champion and that would eventually lead to his murder.

When the Civil War broke out, Catto saw an opportunity to work for the end of slavery and expanded rights for black citizens. On the political front, he went to Washington, DC, and got involved in the inner circles of the Republican Party to push for abolition. He also realized that black contributions to the war effort could build support for equal rights. He raised a volunteer regiment of black soldiers led by white officers, but the army rejected the unit since blacks were not authorized to fight. Edward Stanton, the secretary of war would overrule the army on this point, but by the time that happened the regiment had dispersed back to their homes. Nonetheless, a clear decision had been made that would allow Catto and others to raise troops for the Union cause. He teamed up with Frederick Douglass to raise up eleven black regiments from the Philadelphia area that saw action in the war. Catto himself was given the rank of major, though he never saw combat.

Catto became increasingly committed to the Republican Party during the war as the only hope for blacks to gain equal rights. He joined the Pennsylvania Equal Rights League, a Republican organization dedicated to getting blacks the right to vote. In 1864, he met with black leaders from around the country in Syracuse, New York, for the National Convention of Colored Men. The convention formed the National Equal Rights League, an organization dedicated to promoting racial equality in the United States. Frederick Douglass was elected as the organization's first president.

Catto's troops trained outside Philadelphia, but in areas serviced by the city's horse-drawn trolleys. Unfortunately, however, the trolleys refused to carry black passengers, and so the soldiers' families were unable to visit them. Further, black women and children were often kicked off the trolleys by conductors and white passengers in all kinds of weather. Catto was determined to see this end and was willing to use civil disobedience to achieve his ends. A reporter for the *New York Times* told the story:

## THE RIGHTS OF COLORED CITIZENS.;
### Curious Affair in Philadelphia.

PHILADELPHIA, Wednesday, May 17 [1865] — 2 P.M.

Last evening a colored man got into a Pine-street passenger car, and refused all entreaties to leave the car, where his presence appeared to be not desired.

The conductor of the car, fearful of being fined for ejecting him, as was done by the Judges of one of our courts in a similar case, ran the car off the track, detached the horses, and left the colored man to occupy the car all by himself.

The colored man still firmly maintains his position in the car, having spent the whole of the night there.

The conductor looks upon the part he enacted in the affair as a splendid piece of strategy.

The matter creates quite a sensation in the neighborhood where the car is standing, and crowds of sympathizers flock around the colored man.

Even so, the city would not pass a law prohibiting discrimination against blacks on the trolleys. The following year, Catto proposed a series of resolutions at the Union Club of Philadelphia denouncing the treatment of blacks on the trolleys and calling on whites to stand up for blacks, as part of their Christian duty, when they saw discrimination. One of his resolutions read:

Resolved, That while men and women of a Christian community can sit unmoved and in silence, and see women barbarously thrown from the cars, — and while our courts of justice fail to grant us redress for acts committed in violation of the chartered privileges of these railroad companies, — we shall never rest at ease, but will agitate and work, by our means and by our influence, in court and out of court, asking aid of the press, calling upon Christians to vindicate their Christianity, and the members of the law to assert the principles of the profession by granting us justice and right, until these invidious and unjust usages shall have ceased.

Catto also worked with two US senators to pass a bill in Pennsylvania that prohibited discrimination in transportation across the entire state. When the Philadelphia trolleys continued their old practices, Catto's fiancée, Carolyn Le Count, took the city to court and forced them to comply with the new state law (1867).

The parallels between what Catto did in Philadelphia and what Rosa Parks would do in 1955 in Montgomery, Alabama, are striking. Catto succeeded in desegregating public transportation in Pennsylvania through his civil disobedience in much the same way that Rosa Parks's civil disobedience set in motion the events that led the Supreme Court to outlaw segregation in public transportation nationally.

Along with his academic, political, legal, and military work, Catto was also an athlete. Like many other people in American academia at the time, Catto took up the British sport of cricket, but he switched over to the newly emerging American sport of baseball. Catto was the cofounder of the Pythian Base Ball Club and played shortstop for them. He promoted baseball in the black community so strenuously that Philadelphia would emerge as a major center for Negro League Baseball.

With the support of the white Athletic Base Ball Club, they petitioned to join the new Pennsylvania Base Ball Association in 1868; when it became obvious that they would not be accepted, they withdrew their application. Nonetheless, they challenged many white teams to games, and in 1869 they played the Olympic Ball Club in the first formal baseball game with teams from different races.

On the political and legal front, Catto continued to fight for equal rights for blacks and especially for voting rights.

The Fifteenth Amendment, giving blacks the right to vote, was proposed in 1869 and passed in 1870. Catto spent the time from 1869 to 1871 traveling in Pennsylvania educating blacks about what the amendment would mean for them.

Unfortunately, the prospect of large numbers of black voters—invariably Republican—threatened the political status quo. Irish immigrants, who were closely tied to the Democratic Party, felt especially threatened. They were already competing with blacks for housing and jobs, and now their political power was in jeopardy. In Catto's own precinct, the Fifteenth Amendment could have switched the balance of power away from the Democrats to the Republicans.

The result was large-scale voter intimidation, violence, and riots to prevent blacks from voting. The police, many of whom were Irish, frequently refused to protect blacks or allow them to vote.

Catto was on his way to the polls when Frank Kelly, an associate of the local Democratic Party boss, recognized him. He shot Catto in the back three times and one of the bullets pierced Catto's heart. He was pronounced dead at the police station where his body had been taken.

Catto was given a military funeral, the largest funeral Philadelphia had ever seen.

Kelly escaped to Chicago where he lived in hiding for six years. Eventually he was discovered, arrested, and sent to Philadelphia for trial. Three blacks and three whites who had witnessed the murder identified him as the gunman. Nonetheless, the jury comprised entirely of working-class whites acquitted him.

Unlike Frederick Douglass, Harriet Tubman, and other black heroes in the battle for abolition, Catto has been largely forgotten. He serves as a reminder that not all blacks were slaves in America, yet even those who were not faced discrimination because of their race. In living out his worldview, in insisting on the biblical idea that we are all equal as people made in the image of God, in calling society to order itself according to biblical truth, Catto made important contributions to the development of civil rights in America. His work went well beyond abolition to calling his countrymen to act out the faith they professed.

## SOURCES

Emma Jones Lapsansky, "'Discipline to the Mind': Philadelphia's Banneker Institute, 1854–1872," *Pennsylvania Magazine of History and Biography* 117.1–2 (Jan.–April, 1993): 83–102, https://journals.psu.edu/pmhb/article/view/44836/44557.

Christopher Munden, "Octavius Catto: Philadelphia's 'Forgotten Hero,'" *Constitution Daily*, February 8, 2012, https://news.yahoo.com/news/news/octavius-catto-philadelphia-forgotten-hero-100203556.html.

"Octavius Catto," http://moralheroes.org/octavius-catto.

V. Chapman Smith, "The Triumph and Tragedy of Octavius V. Catto," http://www.ushistory.org/people/catto.htm.

# PANDITA RAMABAI (1858-1922)
## *Mother of Widows and Orphans*

TRADITIONAL SOCIETY IN INDIA WAS not a very welcoming place for girls. Women were considered inferior to men and were not allowed to be educated or to work. Child brides were very common, as were child widows. Even with the abolition of sati, the fate of these widows was harsh: they were considered cursed and were subjected to terrible abuse and even torture at the hands of their husband's family.

Not all Hindu husbands and fathers treated their wives and daughters so badly, however. The unjust treatment of child widows became an issue recognized by Pandita Ramabai, a Hindu scholar whose work to protect widows expanded tremendously after she converted to Christianity.

Pandita Ramabai was the daughter of Anant Shastri, a highly educated Brahmin (the priestly caste in India) who made his living reading the *Puranas* (Hindu Scriptures) in temples. Hinduism teaches that listening to the *Puranas* is a way of earning spiritual merit.

Unlike the vast majority of his peers, Anant Shastri believed that women should be educated. When he was forty years old, he married a nine-year-old girl and taught her Sanskrit. This led to his family and community ostracizing him, so he, his wife, and three children began an itinerant life reading the *Puranas* wherever he could—in temples, during festivals, for wealthy but illiterate Hindu families, etc. This was enough to earn them a modest living, even though they were constantly on the move.

One of the children in the family died young. The other two were an older son named Srinivas and younger daughter named Ramabai. When Ramabai was thirteen, the region was hit by a tremendous famine. People could no longer support the Shastri family, and they began to starve. They tried living off the land, but the parents grew ill. Avant Shastri was the first to succumb to hunger and illness, followed a few months later by his wife. Ramabai and Srinivas were left to fend for themselves.

Ramabai's faith was shaken by these experiences, but she followed in her father's footsteps by reading the *Puranas* and teaching Hinduism. She and her brother made their way to the city of Calcutta where the local Brahmins welcomed them. Ramabai astonished them with her ability to read the *Puranas* and by her mastery of the very difficult grammar of

Sanskrit. She also showed a great deal of wisdom, with the result that the Brahmin community in Calcutta gave her its highest title, *Pandita* (scholar), and invited her to give lectures and to continue her studies.

Her further studies did nothing to confirm her faith, however; she grew increasingly dissatisfied with Hinduism. Then in 1880 her brother took ill and died. Bipen Behan Das Medhavi, a friend of her brother, had sought her hand in marriage for some time. Although he was a lawyer from a lower caste, she followed in her father's footsteps by breaking with tradition and marrying him. This again shocked the Brahmin community, but he did love her and took good care of her. They had a daughter, whom they named Manorama (Joy of the Heart).

Pandita Ramabai noticed a copy of the Gospel of Luke written in Bengali in her husband's library (part of the fruit of William Carey's work). She asked him about it, and he told her he got it at a missionary school. She wanted to know more, so they invited a missionary into their home to explain it to her. She felt drawn to Jesus and wanted to become a Christian, but she knew her husband would not agree to that.

Pandita Ramabai and her husband had planned to start a school for widows, but after they had been married for only eighteen months, her husband contracted cholera and died. As a widow, she was not welcome in her husband's home, so she returned with her daughter to her home territory. She settled in Pune and began to learn English. She wrote her first book there, entitled *Morals for Women*.

One day, a child widow came to her door looking for charity. Pandita Ramabai took her in and treated her like her own daughter. In response to the young widow's situation, Ramabai started an organization called *Arya Mahila Samaj* to educate girls and to advocate for the abolition of child marriage. Unfortunately, she had little money and she realized she needed more training if she was going to be able to fulfill her vision.

Meanwhile, she got to know an English missionary named Miss Hurford. Miss Hurford was returning to England and she urged Ramabai to accompany her. Although Ramabai was afraid of the voyage, she believed God was calling her to go. The sales of *Morals for Women* earned just enough money to book passage for her and for Manorama, so they set sail with Miss Hurford for England.

In England, she heard the story of the woman taken in adultery. This convinced her that Jesus was the greatest liberator of women in history and presented a sharp contrast to Hindu culture. She explained that there were

> only two things on which all those books, the Dharma Shastras, the sacred epics, the Puranas and modern poets, the popular preachers of the present day and orthodox high-caste men, were agreed, that women of high and low caste, as a class were bad, very bad, worse than demons, as unholy as untruth; and that they could not get Moksha, as men.[23]

23. Pandita Ramabai, *A Testimony of Our Inexhaustible Treasure* (1907).

As a result, she converted to Christianity and was baptized in the Anglican church. She would spend the rest of her life living out her faith even as she continued to pursue the vision for widows she had adopted in India.

Pandita Ramabai arranged to teach Sanskrit at Cheltenham College, and in exchange she studied English and education. From there, she traveled to America in 1886 to study the public school system and get some industrial training. She also began networking. She wrote a book entitled *High Caste Hindu Woman* and began giving lectures on the plight of women in India. In 1887, the Americans responded by setting up an association to fund her work. They guaranteed support for her for ten years.

Pandita Ramabai returned to India in 1889. She went to Bombay (modern Mumbai) and within six weeks set up a school for Brahmin girls called *Sharda Sadan* (House of Knowledge). Her friends in Bombay agreed to support her as long as she did not promote Christianity. She agreed, and so the school followed all the rules of the Brahmin caste while remaining nonsectarian. This was the first home for widows in the Bombay area and only the second in India.

But the reformers in Bombay, all of whom were Hindus, were suspicious of Pandita Ramabai's motives and the financial connection with missionaries. Within a year the school was under attack, and given that she allowed the widows to attend prayer meetings, local financial support dried up. She moved the school to Pune, and by 1900, the school had trained eighty women who were able to support themselves through teaching or nursing.

At this point, she realized just how much she needed Christ's help if she was to carry on with her work. She wrote,

> One thing I knew by this time, that I needed Christ and not merely His religion.... I was desperate.... What was to be done? My thoughts could not and did not help me. I had at last come to an end of myself, and unconditionally surrendered myself to the Saviour; and asked Him to be merciful to me, and to become my righteousness and redemption, and to take away all my sin.[24]

Meanwhile, a famine hit the area around Pune in 1897. Plague had also broken out, and so the government of Pune tried to prevent its spread by restricting the movement of people; as a result, the school was limited to one hundred students. But Pandita Ramabai still felt called to care for the widows and girls who were suffering from the famine, so she purchased one hundred acres in Kedgaon, thirty miles from Pune, and started her second school. She called this the Mukti Mission. (*Mukti* means "salvation" in Marathi, the local language.) She soon found 200 girls and child widows and brought them to the new school.

Pandita Ramabai had only two assistants, one Indian and one English. They quickly built huts for the girls and organized a system to take care of them and educate them. They would teach the older ones first, who would then take care of the younger ones. In this way, they managed to care for the

24. Ramabai, *A Testimony.*

growing number of girls who made their way to the school. By 1900, two thousand girls were living there.

The curriculum in these schools included a range of subjects: literature, selected for moral teaching to promote caring; physiology, to teach them about their bodies; botany; and industrial arts such as printing, carpentry, tailoring, masonry, woodcutting, weaving, needlework, farming, and gardening.

Students were also required to join societies such as the Temperance Union or the Christian Endeavour Society to break down caste barriers and to develop relationships based on common interest rather than birth. Pandita Ramabai believed that caste was one of the most serious problems facing India, and she worked very hard to break its power over the culture.

Along with establishing these schools, in 1904, Pandita Ramabai began translating the Bible into Marathi, her native language, from the original Hebrew and Greek; the New Testament was published in 1913, and the complete Bible in 1924.

In 1919, the king of England awarded Pandita Ramabai the Kaisar-i-Hind award, the highest honor that could be given to an Indian during the colonial period.

Pandita Ramabai cared for her girls until her death in 1922. The mission in Pune is still active today.

By common grace, Pandita Ramabai was able to recognize the evils done to women in her culture, yet as a Hindu scholar she found no resources to address them. Once she encountered Jesus in the pages of Scripture, she found in him everything that she had been looking for. He not only treated women with honor and respect, but provided her with the strength and direction to pursue his Kingdom by serving the last, the least, and the lost of India in fulfillment of the vision God had placed in her heart even before she knew him.

# JAMES EMMAN KWEGYIR AGGREY (1875-1927)
## *The Father of African Education*

WHEREVER THE GOSPEL GOES, schools and hospitals follow. The reason is simple: far from being an other-worldly religion, Christianity has historically valued life in this world, and Christians have cared about our minds and bodies. In particular, many of the most important leaders in education in the developing world were Christians and became involved in education because of their Christian commitments. One example is James Emman Kwegyir Aggrey.

James Aggrey was born in Anamabu, a village of the Gold Coast in modern-day Ghana, at a time when the region was a British protectorate. His mother Abna Andu was the daughter of a traditional healer. His father, Kodwo Kwegyir, was sixty when Aggrey was born. Kodwo was a descendant of kings and a prominent elder in the royal court with a well-earned reputation as a warrior and a diplomat.

In 1883, Aggrey converted to Christianity and was baptized into the Wesleyan church, taking the name James. He began attending the Wesleyan missionary school, where he excelled in his studies to such an extent that it soon became obvious to his mother and father that he was a born scholar. He eventually became the school's headmaster.

In 1898, Bishop John Bryan Small from the African Methodist Episcopal Zion church in Barbados arrived in the Gold Coast looking for talented students to send to America for training as missionaries. Aggrey was an obvious choice, and so on July 10 of that year, he set off for the United States.

Aggrey arrived in Salisbury, North Carolina, where he began his studies at Livingston College. He studied a wide range of subjects and graduated in 1902. By this point, he had learned French, German, Latin, and ancient and modern Greek, along with English. The following year, he was ordained as a minister in the African Methodist Episcopal Zion church in Salisbury.

From the beginning of his time in America, Aggrey impressed people with his command of English, particularly because of his race. One man is recorded to have remarked, "He is dark as dark, but very few in America can use English as he can."[25]

---

25. "Bangura, the Hero that Africa Needs," Texas Liberal Arts, https://www.laits.utexas.edu/africa/ads/21.html.

In 1905, Aggrey married Rose Douglas, an African American woman from Virginia; they had four children. That same year, he also began teaching at Livingston College. He continued his studies, however, earning a Doctor of Divinity degree from Hood Theological Seminary in 1912 and a doctorate in osteopathy in 1914. He changed parishes and in 1915 began additional studies at Columbia University, where he studied psychology, sociology, and Japanese.

In 1920, Dr. Paul Monroe, a professor at Columbia and a member of the board of the Phelps-Stokes Fund, offered Aggrey the opportunity to join the otherwise all-white Phelps-Stokes African Education Commission to assess the educational needs in Africa. Aggrey agreed and traveled to Africa in 1920–21. On this trip, he visited areas that are today in the countries of Sierra Leone, Liberia, Ghana, Cameroon, Nigeria, the Democratic Republic of Congo, Angola, and South Africa.

One of Aggrey's most famous illustrations came from one of the 120 lectures he gave in South Africa on this trip. He faced great trouble due to the racial climate in the colony, at times being prevented from entering the venue where he was to speak because of his color. Nonetheless, Aggrey took the abuse with humility and dignity and did his best to rise above it. In one of those lectures, he commented that you could play a melody of sorts with just the black keys on a piano; you could do the same with the white keys. But for full and perfect harmony, you need both. This illustration of the piano keys became an important symbol for racial reconciliation and harmony ever since.

Although Aggrey was proud of his race—he once said, "I am proud of my colour, whoever is not proud of his colour is not fit to live"[26]—but he steadfastly refused to view humanity in terms dictated primarily by race. True, race is a component of our identity and thus is to be valued, but our ultimate worth, according to Aggrey, is that we are made in the image of God, and thus we need to work to develop our fullest potential in honor of that greater identity.

He explained the problems in Africa with a parable:

> A certain man went through a forest seeking any bird he might find. He caught a young bird, brought it home, put it among his fowls and ducks and turkeys, and gave it chicken's food to eat. Five years later, a naturalist came to visit the man, and noticed the bird. He said to the owner: "Look here, this is an eagle, not a chicken." "Yes, you may be right," said the man, "but I have trained it to be a chicken. It is no longer an eagle, it is a chicken, even though it is enormous."
>
> "No," said the visitor, "it is still an eagle; it has the heart of an eagle, and I shall make it soar high to the heavens." "No," said its owner, "it is now a chicken, and it will never fly."
>
> They agreed to test it. The naturalist picked up the bird, held it up, and said loudly: "Eagle, thou art an eagle; thou dost belong to the sky and not down here. Stretch forth thy wings and fly," and with that he hurled the bird up. The eagle turned this way and that, and then looking down, saw the chickens eating, and came to join them.

26. Bangura.

The owner said: "I told you it is now a chicken." "No," said the man, "this bird is an eagle. I shall come back to prove this to you." The exercise was repeated three times, with the same result. The bird always came back to feed with the chickens.

The naturalist came back again, chose a hill, and held the bird aloft, pointing it to the rising sun, and shouted: "Eagle, thou art an eagle; thou dost not belong down here. Thou dost belong to the sky; stretch forth thy wings and fly." The eagle looked round, trembled as if new life was filling it, and suddenly it stretched out its wings, and with the screech of an eagle, it mounted higher, and higher, and never returned. It was really an eagle, though it had been kept and tamed like a chicken!

My people of Africa, we were created in the image of God, but men have made us think that we are chickens, and we still think we are, but we are eagles. Stretch forth your wings and fly! Don't be content with the food of chickens.[27]

When he returned to America, Aggrey toured the United States and Canada giving extemporaneous lectures followed by question-and-answer sessions. In one of these lectures in Canada, Aggrey made one of his most famous statements: "Only the best is good enough for Africa."[28]

In 1924, Aggrey again traveled to Africa with the Phelps-Stokes Commission, this time visiting Ethiopia, Kenya,

27. Bangura.
28. Ibid.

Uganda, Tanzania and Zanzibar, Malawi, Zimbabwe, South Africa, and Ghana. A white South African commented after one of his lectures, "Damn his colour, the man is a saint!"

That same year, Aggrey was appointed the assistant vice principal of Achimota College in Accra, Ghana. (Apparently, the British objected to having a black appointed as the Vice Principal of a school that was originally to be named Prince of Wales College.) Aggrey designed the emblem of the school, which was built around his image of the black and white keys of a piano.

Aggrey became a critically important figure for African education on a tremendous number of levels, so much so that he has been called "the Father of African Education" and "the Booker T. Washington of Africa." His educational philosophy was built around the idea that education was more than just intellectual development or learning a trade: "By education, I do not mean simply learning. I mean training in mind, in morals, and in hand that makes one socially efficient. Not simply the three R's, but the three H's: the head, the hand, and the heart."

Further, he believed that women needed to be educated just as much as men. He was able to convince the colonial government to make the Achimota College coeducational, telling the governor, "The surest way to keep a people down is to educate the men and neglect the women. If you educate a man you simply educate an individual, but if you educate a woman you educate a family."

In 1927, Aggrey returned to the United States to do a preaching and lecturing tour and to complete a book at Columbia

University. Unfortunately, he contracted pneumococcal meningitis. He was admitted into the hospital but died very quickly. He was fifty-two years old. In a mark of just how effective Aggrey had been at spanning the color divide in that racist era, his pall-bearers were all white citizens of Salisbury, North Carolina.

# SOLOMON TSHEKISHO
# PLAATJE (1876-1932)
*Opponent of Apartheid*

DESPITE STEREOTYPES TO THE
contrary, Christians have long been at the forefront of the
push for racial equality. This comes from the Bible's teaching
that the image of God that we all share is the foundation
for human dignity and from the New Testament's insistence
on the spiritual and moral equality of all people. In American history, we see the importance of Christianity in the civil
rights movement in the work of the Rev. Dr. Martin Luther
King, Jr., and of organizations such as the Southern Christian Leadership Conference. Less well known is the work of
African Christians in promoting racial equality in the face

of European colonization of Africa. One example of this is Solomon Plaatje.

To understand Plaatje's career, a brief history of European colonization in South Africa is in order. The indigenous people were primarily speakers of Bantu languages, including for example Shona, Zulu, and Tswana. When Europeans began sailing around Africa to make it to India in the sixteenth century, the region came under the trading domination of the European powers looking to control trade to the Indian Ocean. This began with the Portuguese, who dominated the region without actively colonizing it. They were displaced by the Dutch in 1652, who established the first European colony in the area. With the growing importance of India for the British Empire, the British took over the territory in 1806.

The British established a policy of racial equality (in principle, at least) and eventually abolished slavery. Even though the empire compensated slave owners for the loss of their property, this was too much for many of the Dutch who remained in South Africa. They moved to the interior and established a series of republics run by whites, including the Orange Free State. Eventually, due to the discovery of diamonds and gold in these territories, they were absorbed by the British and incorporated into the Union of South Africa.

Solomon Plaatje was born in the Orange Free State, the sixth of eight boys. His parents were Christians who worked for missionaries around South Africa. The family moved to the British Cape Colony when he was four years old to work for the Lutheran Berlin Mission Society. He was educated in the mission school but was so capable that at age fifteen, he began teaching in the school while continuing his studies privately with the missionaries. Ultimately, he became fluent in seven languages, including English, German, Dutch, and the major African languages of the region.

Plaatje left his teaching position after two years to become a telegraph messenger. He then passed the civil service examinations in Dutch and typing. The Cape Colony allowed anyone who was literate in either English or Dutch and who made fifty pounds per year to vote, so when Plaatje turned twenty-one, he was able to participate in elections. When the Second Boer War broke out, he became an interpreter at the critical Siege of Mafeking. He kept a diary of his experiences in English, which was published after his death.

After the war, since he could no longer advance within the civil service, Plaatje turned to journalism. In 1901 he began publishing the first Setswana-English weekly, *Koranta ea Becoana* (Newspaper of the Tswana), in Mafeking. After editing the paper for six or seven years, he moved to Kimberley, where he started *Tsala ea Becoana* (Friend of the Tswana), later renamed *Tsala ea Batho* (Friend of the People). The name change reflected an important aspect of Plaatje's thinking: he was ardently opposed to tribalism and spent much of his career working to promote African unity and national consciousness. Along with his work on his own newspapers, he also contributed articles to others. Throughout his work as a journalist, he saw his role as being a mouthpiece for his people.

Unfortunately, with the Treaty of Union of South Africa (1910) Plaatje and other blacks lost the right to vote. Plaatje understandably felt betrayed, which helped to set up much of the rest of his career as an activist.

In 1912, in part as a response to the Treaty of Union of South Africa, a number of black leaders formed the South African Native National Congress, which was later renamed the African National Congress (ANC). Because of his leadership in promoting African unity, Plaatje was selected to be its first secretary-general.

The following year, the South African government passed the Natives' Land Act, which restricted the right of blacks ("natives") to own property. This became a cornerstone of apartheid. The South African Native National Congress fought this act and did everything in its power constitutionally to try to have the rights of blacks recognized, but to no avail. When all legal avenues within South Africa were exhausted, they decided to go over the head of the colonial government and appeal to Parliament in London in 1914.

Unfortunately, that was the year World War I broke out, and the government had no time to deal with South Africa. The rest of the delegation returned to South Africa, but Plaatje stayed behind in London until 1917. While there, he lectured, worked as a language assistant at the University of London, and published three books: *Native Life in South Africa*, a denunciation of the 1913 Natives' Land Act; a book of proverbs in his native language with English translation; and a reader in his native language.

After the war, the British government had the opportunity to revisit the issue of the rights of blacks in South Africa. In 1919, Plaatje made a personal appeal to Prime

Minister Lloyd-George, who had also received a submission from the Afrikaner Nationalist delegation headed by General Hertzog. Lloyd-George wrote to General Smuts, the Prime Minister of South Africa, that Plaatje made a much better case than Hertzog, but the British government was unwilling to interfere with the decisions of the all-white South African parliament. And so the system of apartheid remained in place.

Plaatje traveled a great deal in promoting the cause of the black South Africans, including time in Canada and the United States, where he met with Marcus Garvey, W.E.B. Dubois, and the leaders of the NAACP. With their help, he arranged for an American edition of his book, *Native Life in South Africa*. Wherever he went, he won over audiences with his command of language and sense of humor.

As time went on, Plaatje devoted more time to literary activities. He had already written the first English language novel written by an African (*Mhudi: An Epic of South African Native Life a Hundred Years Ago*, written in 1919 but not published until 1930). Returning to London, he began producing translations of Shakespeare's plays into Tswana.

At the end of 1923, Plaatje returned home to South Africa, where he continued to lobby the government on behalf of the native community and to report on the doings of parliament. In 1929, the black community in Kimberley gave him a house at 32 Angel Street to thank him for his service to their people. Although his relationship with the ANC became strained at times, he continued to work with them, including traveling with a delegation to Congo to observe conditions there. He also became involved in a number of other organizations, including the Joint Council movement and the African People's Organization.

In the midst of all his work, he continued to be a committed Christian. For example, in the last period of his life he organized the Christian Brotherhood, a fellowship in Kimberley.

Plaatje contracted pneumonia on a trip to Johannesburg in 1932. He died there and was buried in Kimberley. Over a thousand people attended his funeral. After that, however, he was gradually forgotten. His manuscripts were lost, his works largely unread, and his political activity produced no tangible results. It wasn't until 1970 that he was rediscovered, resulting in a growing interest in his work. The front garden, façade, and two front rooms of his house in Kimberley were declared a national monument in 1992.

Plaatje's career was an outworking of his Christian faith that recognized that all human beings are created in the image of God and thus that they are all equal in dignity and possessed of God-given rights that cannot justly be taken from them. His efforts to overcome tribalism and apartheid both grew from that conviction, as did his burning indignation at the unjust system that had been put into place in his country.

But one other lesson from Plaatje's life is worth noting: he did not appear to have succeeded at all in his work. While recognized as an important leader in his lifetime, he faded quickly into obscurity even as the ANC moved toward radicalism and communism. Yet the principles he worked for eventually resurfaced in the leadership of the ANC, including in Nelson Mandela, as well as in other anti-apartheid leaders such as Archbishop Desmond Tutu and Rev. Allan Boesak. Despite his obscurity, the seeds he sowed eventually bore fruit, which should be a reminder to us that we should not judge our work for God by what we see, but rather by our faithfulness in carrying out his purposes for us.

# CHIUNE SUGIHARA (1900-1986)
## A Bureaucrat Who Saved Jews

IN THE MID- TO LATE-1800s, JAPAN ended its long centuries of isolationism and opened to the outside world. Knowing the de facto loss of sovereignty in China to Western nations in the aftermath of the Opium Wars, Japan decided not to give the industrial powers an excuse to do the same to their country. They rapidly industrialized and patterned their government on superficially Western lines while preserving the existing power structure.

Then they started building their own empire, starting with taking Chinese cities following the model of the Western powers, and then moving on to take Korea and Manchuria (northeast China). After World War I, the Japanese continued to build their empire in China as well as setting their sights on other areas in the Pacific. Given that Britain, France, and the Netherlands all had interests in the western Pacific, the Japanese allied with Hitler on the principle that the enemy of my enemy is my friend.

Although the Japanese had a culture of obedience to superiors and especially to the emperor, at least one man and his wife gave their first allegiance to God over the empire. His name was Chiune Sugihara.

Sugihara was born into a middle-class family in Gifu Prefecture in Japan. His father, who was a physician, intended Chiune to go to medical school. Chiune had other plans, however: he intentionally failed his entrance exams by writing only his name on the tests. Instead of medical school, he entered Waseda University in 1918, where he majored in English. While there, he joined *Yuai Gakusha*, a Christian fraternity.

In 1919 he passed the Foreign Ministry Scholarship exam and was soon sent to Harbin, a city in Manchuria, China, to study German and Russian. He graduated in 1924 with honors and was promptly hired by the Foreign Ministry as deputy foreign minister in Manchuria.

During this period, Sugihara joined the Russian Orthodox church and was baptized as Pavlo Sergeivich Sugihara. He married Klaudia Semionova Apollonova, a Russian woman, though they divorced in 1935 before his return to Japan.

While in Harbin, Sugihara was involved in negotiations with the Soviet Union over the Northern Manchuria Railway. Manchuria was under the control of Japan at this time, and Sugihara was disturbed by the poor treatment of the Chinese. He resigned in protest and returned to Japan.

Back home, Sugihara married Yukiko Kikuchi. The two would have four children. He was sent as a translator for the Japanese legation in Helsinki, Finland, in 1938. In March 1939, he was appointed vice-consul of the Japanese Consulate in Kaunas, Lithuania, where he was expected to report on Soviet troop movements. What he actually did there, however, was far more important.

Kaunas was full of Polish Jewish refugees fleeing the Nazis. One day, Sugihara was in a gourmet food shop. An eleven-year-old boy named Solly Ganor, the nephew of the shop's owner, was also there. His parents were Russian Jewish *menshevik* refugees. Solly was concerned about the fate of Polish Jews and had given all of his money and Hanukah *gelt* (money given as gifts during Hanukah) to aid them. But then he heard that a new Laurel and Hardy movie was showing in town, and so he went to visit his aunt Annushka in hopes of getting a *lit* (Lithuanian dollar) to go to the movie.

Sugihara overheard Solly and offered the boy money. Solly, who had never seen an Asian before, did not know what to make of this offer, so he mumbled that he couldn't accept money from strangers. Sugihara said that he should consider him his uncle for the holiday, and since that made him family, it would be alright to accept the money. Solly looked into the stranger's kind eyes and impulsively said that if he was his uncle, he should come to the family's celebration of the first night of Hanukah, 1939.

Sugihara and his wife were delighted to accept, and so they attended their first Jewish Hanukah celebration. They were warmly welcomed and long remembered the cakes, cookies, and desserts they had at the party.

Most of the evening was a warm celebration of the holiday. But Solly's family was housing a Polish refugee named Mr. Rosenblatt. As the evening wore on, he talked about the slaughter of the Jews in Poland under the Nazis. He tearfully told of the bombing of his house, which killed his wife and children. His story had a tremendous impact on everyone, especially the Sugiharas.

The next day, Solly and his father visited Sugihara at the consulate. They found him phoning the Russians asking for visas to allow the Jews to cross the border.

In summer 1940, the Soviets formally annexed Lithuania. The Jews were desperate to get exit visas to leave the country, and in July Sugihara was awakened by a crowd of hundreds of Jewish refugees standing outside the consulate. Sugihara wired Japan three times asking for permission to issue transit visas for the Jews. (A transit visa would allow the Jews to travel through Japan on their way somewhere else.) Three times he was told not to issue the visas unless they also had visas to go to another country.

Sugihara was in a difficult situation: if he issued the visas, he could be fired and disgraced; if he didn't, the Jews would die. He and Yukiko agreed that they needed to follow their consciences even though they knew it would cost him his position, and the two went to work.

From July 31 to September 4, Sugihara began writing visas by hand at a rate of 300 per day. He didn't even stop for meals—he ate sandwiches that Yukiko left for him by his desk. He even made arrangements for the Soviets to transport them via the Trans-Siberian Railroad (albeit at five times the normal price).

The refugees began to arrive by the thousands begging for visas. When some began to scale the walls of the consulate, Sugihara came out and promised them he would not abandon them.

And he didn't. When he was forced to leave Kaunas before the consulate was closed, Sugihara spent the entire night before writing visas. Eyewitnesses said that he continued to write them on the train, tossing them out of the windows as he completed them. In the end, he simply signed and sealed blank visas to be filled in later.

As he was on the verge of departing, he said, "Please forgive me. I cannot write any more. I wish you the best." He bowed deeply to the crowds, and someone called, "Sugihara, we'll never forget you. I'll surely see you again."

No one knows exactly how many visas Sugihara wrote. Not all were used; some people waited until it was too late to leave. Others were for heads of households, so several people would travel under a single visa. The most commonly accepted number is that 6,000–10,000 Jews escaped the Holocaust because of Sugihara's actions. Today, somewhere between 40,000 and 80,000 people are descendants of the Jews saved by Sugihara.

Many of the refugees joined the Russian Jewish community in Kobe, Japan; others got transit visas organized by the Polish ambassador in Tokyo to a wide range of third countries, including to a Jewish community in Shanghai, China.

The Nazis wanted the Japanese to kill or send back the Jews, but the Japanese ignored their allies. Ironically, Nazi propaganda worked against them here: the Japanese had heard from the Nazis that the Jews were very good with business and finance, and so they thought that having them would be an asset to Japan. The Jews for their part also played up Nazi racism against Asians, which also made the Japanese less inclined to listen to Germany about exterminating the Jews.

Sugihara paid a price for his actions. He was posted to a variety of Eastern European posts during the war and was captured and imprisoned with his family by the Russians for eighteen months. They were released in 1946 and returned to Japan via the Trans-Siberian Railroad. In 1947, the Foreign Ministry asked for his resignation, ostensibly because of post-war downsizing, though some sources have claimed that the Foreign Ministry told them he was forced out because of "that incident" in Lithuania. He lost his youngest son that same year.

Sugihara took a number of menial jobs to support his family. He even resorted to selling light bulbs door to door. Eventually, he was able to use his command of Russian to land a position as an export manager for a Japanese firm in Moscow. He lived there sixteen years, only visiting his family in Japan once or twice a year during that period. He eventually retired to his home in Japan.

After the war, many of the "Sugihara Survivors" tried to locate him, but no one in the Japanese government or the Foreign Ministry seemed to remember him. Finally, in 1968, Joshua Nishri, economic attaché from Israel to Japan and one of the survivors, managed to track him down. All this time Sugihara had no idea whether his actions had saved anyone, and he was surprised and gratified to discover that they had:

he felt that if he had saved even one life all his sacrifices would have been worth it.

The following year, he and his family were invited to Israel, and in 1985, Israel named Sugihara one of the Righteous among the Nations, the highest honor Israel can grant. Sugihara was too ill to attend the ceremony, so Yukiko and their sons accepted the award on his behalf. The family was granted perpetual Israeli citizenship, and one of the sons would eventually graduate from Hebrew University, speaking Hebrew fluently.

Sugihara died the following year. The people of his community in Japan had no idea of what he had done until a delegation from Israel arrived for his funeral.

Sugihara's actions were clearly inspired by his faith. As he told his wife, it was more important for him to obey God than his government. His decision to aid the refugees was particularly influenced by his reading of the book of Lamentations in the Bible. He was a man of remarkable compassion, humility, courage, and faithfulness in carrying out the work that God had uniquely placed him to do.

# HO FENG SHAN (1901-1997)
*Chinese Diplomat for Jews*

ON SEPTEMBER 12, 2015, PRESIDENT
Ma Ying-Jeou of Taiwan posthumously awarded the President's Citation Award to Dr. Ho Feng Shan, honoring for
the first time a man whose courage and compassion had
saved thousands of innocent lives in the years leading up to
World War II.

The recognition was a long time coming.

Ho Feng Shan was born in Yiyang, Hunan province, in
China. His given name (Feng Shan) translates to "Phoenix
on the Mountain." He was orphaned at age seven but was
taken in by Norwegian Lutheran missionaries and educated
in their school. He maintained a lifelong attachment to
Lutheranism: after his retirement in 1973, he immigrated to

San Francisco and became a founding member of the Chinese Lutheran church in the city.

After his early education, Ho traveled to Changsha, the capital of Hunan province, where he attended the elite Yali School. The school had been founded in the 1890s as a preparatory school for Yale-in-China, Yale University's extension college. Upon graduation from Yali, Ho went on to Yale-in-China, and then earned a doctorate *magna cum laude* in political economy from the University of Munich in 1932.

In 1935, Ho joined the diplomatic corps of the Republic of China. His first posting was to Turkey. He had heard that Vienna was a center for European culture, so he wanted to go there. In 1937, he got his chance: he was appointed first secretary to the Chinese legation in Vienna. His fluency in German (as well as English) undoubtedly helped him get this appointment, especially since the ambassador knew French but not German.

Ho quickly began to be involved in the cultural and social life of the city. He was in great demand as a lecturer on Chinese culture and customs.

After the *Anschluss*, when Hitler annexed Austria, all foreign embassies were converted to consulates. Ho was appointed consul general in Vienna, answering to the ambassador in Berlin; the staff at the Vienna consulate was reduced to Ho and one subordinate.

Although Jews had assimilated into Austrian society and Vienna had the third-largest population of Jews in Europe, anti-Semitism was simmering just beneath the surface. The *Anschluss* brought it out in force. Roving gangs of Nazis vandalized Jewish businesses and hauled their owners off to Dachau and other concentration camps. Ho's compassionate nature was deeply offended by the Nazis, and he knew he had to do something to protect the Jews.

Ho recalled, "Since the annexation of Austria by Germany, the persecution of the Jews by Hitler's 'devils' became increasingly fierce. There were American religious and charitable organizations which were urgently trying to save the Jews. I secretly kept in close contact with these organizations. I spared no effort in using any means possible. Innumerable Jews were thus saved."[29]

The "means" he had at his disposal were visas. The Nazis at this time permitted Jews to leave even from concentration camps if they had a visa to another country. The difficulty was that the vast majority of countries refused to give visas to the Jews, presumably out of fear of antagonizing the Nazis.

Ho was not going to let that stop him, however. China had instructed him to be "liberal" with visas, so he began issuing visas that were good only for travel to Shanghai. This was an unusual decision since Shanghai was under partial Japanese occupation at the time and was an open city, that is, no visa was required to go there. In practice, the real purpose of these visas was not so much to allow Jews into Shanghai but to get them out of Austria.

Word spread quickly in the Jewish community that visas were available at the Chinese consulate. People who had

29. Ho Manli, "Diplomatic Rescue: Shanghai as a Means of Escape," November 11, 2005, https://www2.gvsu.edu/walll/ShanghaiMeansofEscape.pdf.

been turned down at other consulates were welcomed by Ho and given visas.

While many traveled to Shanghai on Ho's visas, others ended up in other countries such as the Philippines, Cuba, Canada, and Palestine. He issued visas that covered entire families, in at least one case numbering as many as twenty people.

One particularly memorable story involved the Doran family. Lilith-Silvia Doron bumped into Ho when Hitler was making his triumphal entry into Vienna on March 11, 1938. She explains, "Ho, who knew my family, accompanied me home. He claimed that, thanks to his diplomatic status, they [the Nazis] would not dare harm us as long as he remained in our home. Ho continued to visit our home on a permanent basis to protect us from the Nazis."[30]

Things took a turn for the worse when Doron's brother Karl was arrested and sent to Dachau. Ho issued a visa for the family, and when it was presented to the authorities, Karl was released. The family left immediately and immigrated to Palestine.

Ho faced real challenges as he worked to save the Jews. His family was with him, and he was well aware that the Nazis might ignore his diplomatic immunity if they decided he was too much trouble. His consulate was in a building owned by a Jew, and when it was confiscated by the Nazis Ho rented another using his own money. He also on at least one occasion faced down an armed Gestapo officer to protect a Jewish family.

30. Geng Shan Ho, Holocaust Memorial Day Trust, https://www.hmd. org.uk/resource/feng-shan-ho/

He also had problems with his own ambassador. The Republic of China wanted to maintain good relations with Hitler, and Chen Jie, the Chinese ambassador to Berlin and Ho's superior, ordered him to stop giving Jews visas. Ho replied that the Foreign Ministry—Chen's superiors—had told him to maintain a liberal visa policy, so he would continue. Chen was furious and sent an inspector to Vienna to investigate a trumped-up charge that Ho was selling the visas. Chen evidently could not figure out what Ho was getting out of the visas and assumed there had been kickbacks. There was no evidence of wrongdoing, however. Ho pointed out that the visas were free, so why would anyone pay for them? The inspector returned to Berlin, and all Chen could do was put a negative report into Ho's record for his insubordination.

No one knows the total number of visas Ho issued. He had issued 300 by June 1938; visa number 1906 was signed on October 27, 1938. He continued issuing visas until he was recalled in May 1940. The total number is conservatively estimated to have been around 4,000. How many were used is also unknown, but there is no question that Ho's actions saved thousands of lives.

In 1947, Ho became ambassador to Egypt, a position he held until 1956. When the Communists won the Chinese Civil War and the Nationalists withdrew to Taiwan, Ho remained loyal to the Nationalist cause. After his time in Egypt, he also served as the Republic of China's ambassador to Mexico, Bolivia, and Columbia.

His final posting was marred by a controversy over embassy finances. One of his subordinates, whom Ho had turned down for a promotion, accused him of misappropriating $300 of embassy funds. The accusation was false, and Ho provided proof of his innocence, but political machinations nonetheless led to the end of his career. He was pushed out of the Foreign Service in 1973 and denied a pension after forty years of service to the Republic of China.

Ho retired to San Francisco, where he dedicated himself to his church and to community service. He was a trustee of the Yale-China Association and wrote a memoir entitled *Forty Years of My Diplomatic Life.* The book spends very little time on his efforts to save the Jews and he never spoke about it to anyone. His daughter only pieced the story together after he died.

Ho passed away on September 28, 1997. His daughter brought his ashes to China and buried them in his hometown of Yiyang. The Communist government sent a wreath; the Nationalist government did not even mention his passing.

What made Ho work so hard at such great personal risk to save the Jews when other diplomats, with only rare exceptions, did not? His own answer is compassion; in his own words, "I thought it only natural to feel compassion and to want to help. From the standpoint of humanity, that is the way it should be."

There is more to be said, though. His pastor, Rev. Charles Kuo, commented about him: "He knew he had received many gifts from God. He felt that they were not given to him solely for his own benefit, but to do for others, for his fellow man."[31] Ho said as much himself in a poem written to his wife Shauyun on New Year's Day, 1947:

> The gifts Heaven bestows are not by chance
> The convictions of heroes not lightly formed.
> Today I summon all spirit and strength,
> Urging my steed forward ten thousand miles.[32]

Drilling down even further, we see three interlocking influences in his thinking: his Christian faith; Western liberal education, itself the product in many ways of Christianity; and Confucianism. In fact, he named his children after two tenets taken from Confucius's *Analects*, Virtue and Decorum. These three influences produced a man providentially prepared and sent to Vienna to save lives even at great risk to himself and his family.

Taiwanese recognition of Ho's remarkable efforts in Vienna is thus well deserved if long delayed. Even though they do not seem to have acquitted him of the career-ending accusation of misappropriation of funds, they have gone a long way toward vindicating a true hero.

31. "Feng-Shan Ho: Righteous among the Nations!," About, https://fengshanho.weebly.com/about.html.

32. Ibid.

# ANDRÉ AND MAGDA
## TROCMÉ (1901-1971, 1901-1996)
## & THE VILLAGE OF LE
## CHAMBON-SUR-LIGNON
*Huguenots for the Jews*

LE CHAMBON-SUR-LIGNON IS A SMALL
village in south-central France. Along with the surrounding
villages, the total population of the area was about 5,000 in
the 1940s. Yet these villages, under the leadership of their
Huguenot (French Protestant) pastor André Trocmé and his
wife Magda, were responsible for saving up to 5,000 Jews from
deportation to concentration camps during World War II.

André Trocmé was born in 1901. During World War I, he
developed pacifist sentiments from meeting a young German

pacifist who had come to Le Chambon looking for a place he could live in peace without participating in the war. Trocmé was eventually ordained in the French Protestant church. In 1938, he and fellow pastor Edouard Theis founded the Collège Lycée International Cévenol, a pacifist school that was intended to prepare country students for university studies.

In 1940, France was overrun by the Nazis and a collaborationist government was set up in the French city of Vichy. That winter, a woman came to their door. She was a German Jew fleeing the Nazis, and she thought perhaps the pastor would help her. The Trocmés took her in and fed her, and Magda realized the woman would need false identity documents to avoid capture. The next day, Magda approached the mayor to obtain the false papers, but he was concerned that if a German Jew were found in Le Chambon, the local Jewish community would suffer for it. As a result, he refused to issue the papers. Magda was devastated. She did what she could, giving the woman food and the names of some people who might be able to help her, but she was forced to send her away the next day.

Inspired by this incident, Pastor Trocmé began to exhort his congregation to shelter the "People of the Book" who were fleeing Nazi persecution. He told them, "We shall resist whenever our adversaries demand of us obedience contrary to the orders of the gospel."[33] He led them in a variety of symbolic resistance activities—the staff of the school refused

33. "Andre Trocmé," Plough, https://www.plough.com/en/authors/t /andre-trocme.

to pledge unconditional obedience to the head of state, and he refused to ring the church bells to celebrate Vichy leader Marshal Petain's anniversary—but he was particularly concerned about protecting the refugees who were coming into the area from France, Germany, and Central Europe.

The Trocmés began to organize an underground network to protect the refugees and provide for them. The Collège Lycée International housed children, and the Trocmés identified families who would be willing to take Jews in. Magda was particularly active in making the arrangements, picking up Jews at the train station, and seeing that they were taken care of. When Jews arrived in Le Chambon, André would announce from the pulpit that X number of "Old Testaments" had arrived and ask his congregation who would be willing to take them. There were always volunteers.

Whenever the Nazis came through, the Jews went into the countryside; one villager later explained, "As soon as the soldiers left, we would go into the forest and sing a song. When they heard that song the Jews knew it was safe to come home."[34]

Some of the Jews stayed in Le Chambon for the duration of the war; others were smuggled out, usually to Switzerland, on secret paths through the mountains known only to the locals. We will return to these paths later.

The Vichy government had a good idea of what was going on. They demanded that Trocmé stop his activities. His response

34. "A Town of Righteous Gentiles," International Fellowship of Christians and Jews, October 27, 2021, https://www.ifcj.org/news/stand-for-israel-blog /le-chambon-sur-lignon-a-town-of-righteous-gentiles.

was to the point: "These people came here for help and shelter. I am their shepherd. A shepherd does not forsake his flock. I do not know what a Jew is. I only know human beings."[35]

1942 saw the beginning of mass deportation of Jews to concentration camps. Trocmé urged his congregation to take in any Jews that came seeking help. In August, the Vichy government sent gendarmes to Le Chambon to round up the Jews that they knew (or suspected) were hiding in the area. Trocmé preached a fiery sermon on Deuteronomy 19:2–10, which discusses the right of the persecuted to shelter, and urged his parishioners to "do the will of God and not of men." The gendarmes left without finding a single Jew. In fact, during the war no Jews were captured in the Le Chambon area.

Not all the Jews connected to the Trocmés were so fortunate. André Trocmé's cousin Daniel Trocmé was sheltering Jews in a school in Verneuil, about 400 kilometers from Le Chambon. The Gestapo raided the school in 1943 and found the Jews. Daniel was not there but turned himself in since he believed it was his duty not to abandon those he had sheltered. He died at the Majdanek death camp in 1944.

André himself was arrested in February 1943, along with Edouard Theis and the headmaster of the school. They were taken to a detention camp near Limoges. The commandant demanded that Trocmé sign a document committing him to obey all government orders. He refused. Nonetheless, he

---

35. "Under the Wings of the Church: Protestant Pastor Andre Trocme," I *Am* My Brother's Keeper, 2002, https://www.yadvashem.org/yv/en/exhibitions/righteous/trocme.asp.

was released after five weeks of imprisonment. When he was returned home, he went underground, but the community continued its work even without his visible leadership. Many Jews were thus saved and given the opportunity to live a relatively peaceful life through the end of the war.

Virtually all the people in the region were involved in the effort one way or another, yet not a single person said a word about it to the Nazis.

How do we explain the "conspiracy of goodness" at Le Chambon? The people in the area were taking great personal risks to save strangers of a different religion and had the potential for great reward if they would betray the Jews to the authorities, yet no one did so. Why?

At its most basic level, the answer is that they simply believed it was the right thing to do. A documentary entitled *Weapons of the Spirit* interviewed some of the old people of the village to try to figure out why they did what they did. It is fascinating to watch the reaction. The couple that was interviewed was clearly uncomfortable in front of the camera, and it was obvious that on some level they did not even understand the question: it was the right thing to do, so why wouldn't they do it? As another villager commented, "We didn't protect the Jews because we were a moral or heroic people. We helped them because it was the human thing to do."[36]

Yet so many others did not do "the human thing."

---

36.  "An Unexpected Sanctuary," Pulitzer Center, June 29, 2018, https://pulitzercenter.org/projects/unexpected-sanctuary.

Another aspect of this is the history of the Huguenots in this region. Many Calvinist churches have been philosemitic (that is, they were pro-Jewish). The Huguenots even called their churches "temples" and strongly identified with the Jews because of their own history of persecution.

In the sixteenth century, there were a series of wars of religion in France between the Catholics and the Huguenots. King Henry IV tried to resolve the religious problem by issuing the Edict of Nantes (1598), which gave the Huguenots limited rights to worship. After his death, the terms of the edict were steadily eroded. Louis XIV persecuted the Protestants so badly that many ended up converting to Catholicism to save themselves and their livelihood. Then in 1685, Louis XIV revoked the Edict of Nantes on the grounds that there were no more Huguenots left in the country.

In actuality, there were about one million Huguenots left. They went underground, establishing what they called the Church of the Desert in memory of the wanderings of Israel in the wilderness following the Exodus.

In the area around Le Chambon, the Huguenots made secret rooms similar to the priest holes in England, and secret paths through the mountains to Switzerland to smuggle pastors and Bibles into France. Even after Protestantism was legalized, the people of the area kept the locations of these rooms and paths secret since they never knew when they would need them again.[37] They were put back into service to save the Jews from the Nazis.

The strong moral sense of the people of Le Chambon, fortified by their philosemitism and their history as a persecuted people, provided the motivation for their resistance to the Nazis and rescue of the Jews. The secret rooms and paths were providentially available to them for this task.

After the war, Pastor Trocmé continued his ministry and his promotion of Christian pacifism. He was active in the International Fellowship of Reconciliation, and during the Algerian War, he and Magda set up a group called Eirene (Greek for "peace") in Morocco to help French conscientious objectors.

André Trocmé died in 1971; his wife Magda died in 1996. Both of them and Daniel Trocmé were named among the Righteous among the Nations by the Yad Vashem, the Holocaust Martyrs' and Heroes' Memorial Authority in Jerusalem.

37. Even today, the villagers in the area deny these paths and rooms exist; if they get to know and trust you, they will admit it but will not show them to you since they might need them again in the future.

# MADATHILPARAMPIL
# MAMMEN THOMAS (1916-1996)
## *Christian Leader in Modern India*

ALTHOUGH WE THINK OF CHRISTI-
anity as a Western religion, there are Christian churches in
Asia that are older than most of those in Europe. One example is the Mar Thoma church in India.

Even before the Roman Empire, there was extensive trade
between India and the Mediterranean region. By the first
century AD, Jewish merchants had founded communities in
Malabar in India. According to tradition, in 52 AD Thomas
the Apostle traveled to India and evangelized this area.
Thomas may have picked Malabar for his work because of
the numerous Jewish communities there, or perhaps he was
more successful in evangelizing the region because of those

communities. Either way, he converted a significant number of people and appointed teachers and elders to lead them. He then moved on to Tamil Nadu, where he was martyred.

Around the third century, Syrian Christians from the church of the East, which followed Nestorian doctrine, immigrated into the Malabar area from the Persian Empire and heavily influenced the indigenous churches. Among other things, they brought the Syriac language with them, and that replaced Hebrew as the church's language. The Malankara church, as it came to be called, formalized its place under the jurisdiction of the patriarch of the church of the East around A.D. 650.

The church of the East had an enormous and largely unrecognized impact on Asia, and was arguably the center of world Christianity for the first millennium. As time went on, however, it faced numerous problems. Distance, the expansion of Islam, and political unrest cut India off from the church's center in Mesopotamia in the eleventh century. Relations were not restored until 1301. Later that century, however, the church of the East's hierarchy in Asia largely collapsed, leaving India without a bishop until the church of the East appointed two in the 1490s.

Such was the situation when the Portuguese arrived in 1498, looking to take control of the spice trade. The Malabar Christians were heavily involved in the spice trade themselves and so prospered economically, but they were under pressure from the various Indian states in the area. As a result, they initially welcomed the support of the Portuguese, who for their part saw an alliance with the Malabar Christians as an asset to their bid to take over the spice trade.

Over time, however, the Portuguese began to interfere with the Malankara church. They blocked all connection with the church of the East and with the Eastern Orthodox patriarch of Antioch, even preventing new bishops from being appointed. When the last Metropolitan (i.e., senior bishop) died, the Portuguese pressured the church to convene the Synod of Diamper (1599). This synod placed the Malankara church under the authority of the Portuguese archbishop of Goa and forced it to adopt liturgical and structural reforms. Some of these, such as the abolition of caste distinctions, made sense theologically but hurt the Christians' standing with their Hindu neighbors. Others, such as the burning of books including the *Peshita* (the Syriac translation of the Bible) were little more than a power play on the part of the archbishop to force submission to Rome.

This action led to increasing tensions between the Indian Christians and the Portuguese, until in 1653 the native believers had enough. They gathered together and took the Great Oath of the Bent Cross (so called because the crucifix on which it was sworn bent under the weight of the number of people laying hands on it) that cut the ties between the Malabar Christians and the church of Rome. The church eventually became known as the Mar Thoma church.

When the British took over India, they generally did not interfere with Indian religious affairs. Possibly due to the influence of Anglican missionaries, the leader of the Mar Thoma church established a committee in 1818 to propose reforms for the church. The Reformation formally began in 1836. It eliminated a number of practices (veneration of saints and icons, for example) that were not found in Scripture and affirmed orthodox Christology, while at the same time maintaining traditional liturgies, though in the vernacular rather than in Syriac.

The reforms proved to be very controversial, but over time they were adopted. As the church now sees it, just as the Anglican church is a Western Reformed church, the Mar Thoma church is an Eastern Reformed church.

Madathilparampil Mammen (M.M.) Thomas was born to a Mar Thoma family in 1916. His father, a printer and social activist, was very involved in both the Mar Thoma reformation and the early phases of the Indian independence movement.

M.M. (as he was generally called) graduated with a gold medal in chemistry from Kerala University in 1935. He took a position teaching at a Mar Thoma high school in Perambavoor for two years. In 1937, he turned down high-paying positions to start an orphanage in Trivandrum, the capital of Kerala. At the orphanage, he taught the students technological skills to make them useful and productive citizens.

Like his father, M.M. was involved in the Indian independence movement. He was particularly influenced by Gandhi at this point in his career. He was also influenced by Marxism. In fact, he applied for membership in the Communist party at the same time he applied for ordination in the Mar Thoma church. The Communists turned him down because of his involvement with Christianity; the church turned him down because of his involvement with the Communists. It turns out the Communists were closer to the truth: in all of his work, whether in the independence movement or in social and political activism, he was always guided by his faith.

With only a college degree in chemistry, M.M. began to teach himself theology. But for him, theology was not simply an academic discipline: it had personal, social, and political dimensions as well. One key turning point in his life came when his wife died of cancer. Rather than becoming bitter, he learned at this point in a profound way the importance of the sovereignty of God. Whenever his youngest brother, M.M. Ninan, faced struggles in his life, M.M. asked him, "Who is important? You or God?" Rather than focus on himself, M.M. saw God's sovereignty as ultimately more important than his own difficulties and loss.

He was also concerned with the theological implications of the revolutions of the post-colonial era. He turned away from the Gandhism and Marxism of his youth, though he continued to appreciate the issues that motivated them. For M.M., the Gospel was not found in personal devotion or behind church walls, but in technology, in society, in working for justice and social change, indeed in revolution though not in revolutionary ideologies.

M.M. was also an important figure in the ecumenical movement. He was at the founding meeting of the World Council of Churches, was an active member of the World Conference of Church and Society, and from 1968–1975 was the moderator for Central Committee of the World Council of Churches.

In 1957, he formed the Christian Institute for the Study of Religion and Society with P. D. Devanandan, India's leading theologian. The institute produced a tremendous body of literature on church and society in India, including works on social policy, cultural encounter, Christian-Hindu relations, political analysis, family problems, and ecumenical affairs. M.M. also wrote many works of his own in both Malayalam and English.

After his retirement from the institute, M.M. became a visiting professor of ethics, mission, and ecumenics at Princeton Seminary. He taught one semester a year for six years between 1980 and 1987. This is especially remarkable in view of the fact that he was self-taught as a theologian and his only academic degree was his B.S. in chemistry.

He also continued his involvement in politics. He opposed Indira Gandhi's suspension of democracy in 1976 at great personal risk; his courage in taking this stand eventually led to his appointment as governor of Nagaland, a largely Christian state in northeast India, in 1991. He resigned in 1993, however, in protest of the corruption of the Indian government.

M.M. passed away in 1996 at his home in Kerala.

The Mar Thoma church and M.M. Thomas should remind us that Christianity is not an exclusively Western phenomenon. The church has a long history in Asia, and the impact of Asian Christians continues to the present. For all the influences of Marxism and liberal Christianity on M.M., he remains an example of a man thoroughly committed to the Christian faith of his youth, who sought to live it out in the world as a lay theologian, social activist, and political leader.

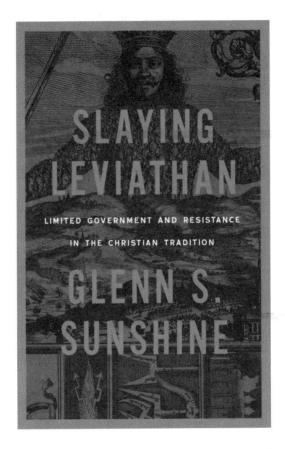

Christians first expressed these political truths under Cae-
sars, kings, popes, and emperors. We need them in the age of
presidents.

Leviathan is rising again, and the first weapon we must
recover is the longstanding Christian tradition of resisting

governmental overreach. Our bloated bureaucratic state would have been unrecognizable to the Founders, and our acquiescence to its encroachments on liberty would have infuriated them. But here is the point: our Leviathan would not have surprised them. They were well acquainted with the tendency of governments to turn tyrannical: "Eternal vigilance is the price we pay for liberty."

In *Slaying Leviathan*, historian Glenn S. Sunshine surveys some of the stories and key elements of Christian political thought from Augustine to the Declaration of Independence. Specifically, the book introduces theories of limited government that were synthesized into a coherent political philosophy by John Locke. Locke, of course, influenced the American founders and was, like us, fighting against the spirit of Leviathan in his day. But his is only one of the many stories in this book.

Title: *Slaying Leviathan: Limited Government and Resistance in the Christian Tradition*
ISBN-13: 978-1952410727

Find *Slaying Leviathan* at www.canonpress.com or listen to the audiobook on Canon+ at mycanonplus.com.